W0013689

Heinemann
ASSEMBLY
Resources

VALUES
for
TODAY

Chris Wright

Heinemann Educational Publishers

Halley Court, Jordan Hill, Oxford OX2 8EJ

a division of Reed Educational & Professional Publishing Ltd

Heinemann is a registered trademark of Reed Educational & Professional Publishing Ltd

OXFORD MELBOURNE AUCKLAND
JOHANNESBURG BLANTYRE GABORONE
IBADAN PORTSMOUTH NH (USA) CHICAGO

Text © Chris Wright, 2000

Copyright notice
All rights reserved. No part of this publication may be reproduced in any material form
(including photocopying or storing it in any medium by electronic means and whether or not
transiently or incidentally to some other use of this publication) without the prior written
permission of the copyright owner, except in accordance with the provisions of the Copyright,
Designs and Patents Act 1988 or under the terms of a licence issued by the Copyright Licensing
Agency, 90 Tottenham Court Road, London W1P 0LP. Applications for the copyright owner's
written permission to reproduce any part of this publication should be addressed to the
publisher.

First published 2000

ISBN 0 435 302353 001

04   03   02   01   00
10   9   8   7   6   5   4   3   2   1

British Library Cataloguing in Publication Data

Cover and inside design by Brian Melville, Big Red Hat Design

Typeset by TechType, Abingdon, Oxon

Printed and bound in Great Britain by Biddles Ltd, Guildford

Acknowledgements
The authors and publishers would like to thank the following for use of copyright material:

The Center for Spiritual Exchange for the extracts from *Taking Flight* by Anthony de Mello, Image
Books, 1988, on pp. 13, 16, 17 and 93-4; The Central Conference of American Rabbis for the
poem 'Gates of Repentance' by Shaarei Teshuva on pp. 34-5, reproduced from *The Union
Prayerbook for the Days of Awe*, ed. Chaim Stern, 1999; *The Daily Mail*, 16 July 1999, for the
extract on pp. 184-5; Defence for Children International for permission to reproduce the *UN
Convention on the Rights of the Child* on pp. 243-7; Express Newspapers for the extract on pp.
126-7; the Gale Group for the extract from *Rosa Parks: The Movement Organizes* by Kai Friese,
Silver Burdett Press, 1990, on pp. 20-3; Lt. Col. Dave Grossman for the extracts from 'Trained to
Kill', reproduced from *Christianity Today*, 10 August 1998: also available by Dave Grossman,
Stop Teaching our Kids to Kill: A Call to Action Against TV, Movie & Video Game Violence,
Crown Publishers (a division of Random House); © Emile Servan-Schreiber 1999, letter to the
International Herald Tribune, 1 October 1998, on p. 124; Little, Brown & Co (UK) for the extracts
from *The Tenth Circle of Hell* by Rezak Hukanovic, Abacus, 1998, on pp. 226-7; ©Telegraph
Group Limited, London 1999, for the quotes on pp. 113, 123 and 192; TIME Magazine, Time Life
Syndication for the quotes on p. 124 and 141; ©Times Newspapers Limited, 12th September
1998, for the quote on p.124; ©Times Supplements Limited for the quote on p.2 and the United
Nations Centre for Human Rights for permission to reproduce the *Declaration of Human Rights*
on pp. 237-42. All Scripture quotations, unless otherwise noted, are from the *Good News Bible*
published by The Bible Societies/HarperCollins*Publishers* Ltd., UK, ©American Bible Society,
1966, 1971, 1976, 1992.

Tel: 01865 888058 www.heinemann.co.uk

The publishers have made every effort to trace the copyright holders, but if they have
inadvertently overlooked any, they will be pleased to make the necessary arrangements at the
first opportunity.

Contents

Contents

Contents

5. Big questions

Appendices

Part 1

Introduction

Introduction

> *The preservation or loss of a nation depends upon the depth or shallowness of its virtue, not upon its strength or weakness.*
>
> (Su Shih, 1036–1101, Chinese government official)
>
> *When I think about what's been going on in America, when you know of what's been going on in Kosovo, we seem to be at the end of our Millennium sinking back to a kind of barbarism. It's terrifying, and we really need as a society to take a very long look at ourselves as to what values we are giving to our people and how we are bringing up our young.*
>
> (Cardinal Basil Hume, 1923–1999, late Archbishop of Westminster)

This book is written at a time when the National Curriculum is being revised and greater attention is being directed to what it means:

(a) to promote the spiritual, moral, and cultural development of pupils; and
(b) to prepare pupils for the opportunities, responsibilities and experiences of adult life (Education Reform Act, 1988).

Ongoing concern over the moral and emotional development of pupils links into the first strand of the Act, whilst government moves to make citizenship education compulsory is aimed at the second strand.

(a) Promoting the moral development of pupils

Since the 1988 Education Reform Act, 'values education' has become of greater concern to each successive government. The Conservative government expressed this concern within the context of a Christian heritage agenda in which collective worship

Introduction

took a pivotal role. The present government's agenda is that of the active citizen who needs to balance rights and responsibilities. The Education Secretary, Mr Blunkett, has said that citizenship lessons would 'help young people develop a full understanding of their duties and responsibilities in a modern democracy as well as their rights, enabling them to play a full role in the life of their communities.' (quoted in *The Times Educational Supplement*, 14 May 1999)

During the writing of this book newspapers and the television brought us pictures of the tragedies of the Columbine High School Massacre in Denver, Colorado, coupled with the NATO bombings of Kosovo and Belgrade and the nail bombings in Brixton and Soho. The culmination of these events has led some leaders to fear that the world is in the grip of a moral crisis. *Values for Today* addresses this need for 'values education'. It is unapologetically about values to which people can aspire.

Promoting moral intelligence

Moral intelligence can be defined as a person's ability to reflect upon what it means to be a 'good person', as opposed to a 'not-so-good person' or a 'bad person'. In the past, this quality was called 'character'. People don't learn moral intelligence by memorizing lists of rules or entering into abstract discussions. However, moral intelligence does involve a person's reasoning capacities. It has to do with considering the complex and ambiguous nature of many issues and discussing multiple points of view. At its heart moral intelligence is concerned with the ability to reflect on values – both inwardly and outwardly. *Values for Today* encourages young people to talk and think about values and moral issues.

Teenagers are looking for goals and direction in life. As they try to work out a value system by which to live, they are – at times – bombarded by conflicting moral signals. Young people take in values from the world, from the consumerist enticements of television, from the music they listen to and from the fashion and magazine industries.

St Francis of Assisi said, 'preach the gospel, use words if necessary'. It is true that the most persuasive moral teaching people do is by example, the witness of their lives, the way they relate to one another, speak to one another and treat one another. Young people are ever-attentive witnesses of adult morality. They are constantly at work noticing what is just and what is unkind, rendering their judgements. They look for clues on how to behave, what is acceptable and what is unacceptable, from a word here, a gesture there, an action praised, an emotion denounced. They find their heroes and saints in their own homes, their schools and from the media. Are they generous or are they selfish? Do they look out for others or are they wrapped up in their own world? The people among whom they live – including teachers – act as their moral agents.

Teachers need to provide moral leadership. If they do not provide this moral compass, they are offering their pupils lessons in indifference and moral apathy, and ultimately lessons that lead to moral confusion. Schools have the responsibility of creating, in W.H. Auden's phrase, 'a whole climate of opinion' which provides a clear sense of what the school stands for, which forms of behaviour are acceptable and which are unacceptable. This is often what is meant by the term 'a school's ethos'. 'Values' or 'character education' is going on all the time, albeit mainly in an informal manner and not as part of the structured curriculum of the school. It will become clear to pupils as they witness the things on which the school comments – which news stories it chooses to remark upon and which it chooses to overlook. Day-to-day life in school becomes its own character-in-action lesson for pupils: what teachers say, why they say it, what they do and how they speak of what they do, if they speak about it.

Promoting emotional intelligence

It is possible to 'get all A's' and flunk life.
(*The Second Coming*, Walker Percy)

Introduction

Emotional intelligence is concerned with how people deal with their own and others' emotions. It has been called 'the most desirable Nineties quality', a fact which is recognized more and more at job interviews where interviewers are as concerned to discover how a candidate will work with others and handle pressure as they are to explore job-specific competencies. Today people are expected to have a high degree of self-awareness, to know their own strengths and limitations and to be able to set personal targets for improvement.

Recent surveys reveal a worldwide trend for the present generation of children to have more emotional problems than the last. They are more depressed, angry and unruly; more prone to worry, more impulsive and aggressive. There is a need to educate young people into using their emotions intelligently. This means making emotions and social life themselves topics for class discussion, rather than treating them as intrusions on the 'real work of the curriculum'. By doing so schools are providing pupils with basic lessons for living that they may not get otherwise. In so doing schools fulfil the mandate of the National Curriculum which aims at preparing pupils for the 'opportunities, responsibilities and experiences of adult life'.

Emotional intelligence can make a great difference in building up and preserving relationships (both at home and work), and reacting well to the vicissitudes of life. A high IQ is no guarantee of achieving happiness in life. It offers very little preparation for the rough and tumble which life sometimes brings. Pupils need to be coached in emotional intelligence and provided with the emotional competencies necessary to handle the emotional roller-coaster well. *Values for Today* offers the classroom teacher material that deals directly with handling the emotions.

(b) Preparing for the opportunities, responsibilities and experiences of adult life: Education for citizenship

Values for Today intends to make a contribution to the government's citizenship initiative. Citizenship education will become a statutory entitlement in secondary schools from 2002. It has formed part of the government's 'unfulfilled agenda' set by the 1988 Education Reform Act, that set education within the context of the spiritual, moral, cultural, mental and physical development of pupils. It stated that the National Curriculum should prepare 'pupils for the opportunities, responsibilities and experiences of adult life'. Citizenship education is part of the preparation for adult life.

The QCA report *'Education for citizenship and the teaching of democracy in schools'* mentions three strands in citizenship education: social and moral responsibility, community involvement and political literacy. It will enable pupils to participate in society effectively as active, informed and responsible citizens, by encouraging them to become involved in public affairs as people who have rights as citizens. It will encourage pupils to take part in public debate that recognizes the increasingly complex nature of our society and encourages sensitivity to ethnic and cultural diversity. Representative democracy should offer respect both to individuals and to the social groups to which they belong. Recent events have highlighted the need, for example, of greater sensitivity to and awareness about racist divisions within British society.

The report recognizes the significant contribution that citizenship learning can make to the development of values. For this reason the first main section of readings (Part 2) in *Values for Today* is concerned with personal values. Parts 3 and 4 consider the needs, rights and responsibilities of people in society: how we respect others and the natural world. As young people prepare to become citizens of a democratic society they need to learn what it means to be responsible and caring actors in their 'global village', whose decisions make a difference. Part 5 explores some of the 'big questions' in life, and has a more philosophical feel to it. Appendices A and B contain value statements from the United Nations. The first, the *Universal Declaration of Human Rights* (Appendix A) is a statement about the basic rights each human being should have. The second, the *UN Convention on the Rights of the Child* (Appendix B) covers

Introduction

everything from a child's right to be free from sexual and economic exploitation, to the right to his or her own opinion, and to the right to education, health care and economic opportunity.

'Are you sitting comfortably? Then we'll begin': The role of stories

In the past children were taught about national heroes and religious saints, people who exemplified virtues. Today, young people's heroes are more likely to be sports persons and pop stars. They live through their favourite soap operas and soak in the moral and emotional messages that these programmes broadcast.

The stories in *Values for Today* have been chosen with two aims in mind: firstly, to show what heroic values look like in practice; secondly, to encourage a more reflective approach to the world and its portrayal in the media. The stories are not simply 'Once upon a time' fictions. They are not 'what might have been' but are there to encourage 'what might be'. These stories are ways to imagine what the world could be like if the values implicit in the stories were practised.

Many of them are character sketches that provide a basis for morality. The stories act as mirrors: through listening to other people's stories we can hear things about ourselves and see things that we might not have thought about before. Stories have this ability to touch us at our deepest levels. They ask the reader, 'What do you think? How does the story make you feel?' The best stories, therefore, have a transformational quality with the ability to disturb, challenge and inspire. Many of the values advocated in the stories link in with the 'concepts, values and dispositions' being advocated in citizenship education.

The setting

Each of the readings in this book is divided into four parts: a theme, an introduction, the reading – usually a story – and a pause for reflection.

Theme: a statement introducing the value, disposition or attitude being explored in the reading. This is mainly intended for teacher reference.

Introduction: a quote, comment or statement introducing the theme and context of the reading. It is intended to start pupils thinking about the topic. Occasionally the introduction will also include an activity.

Reading: sometimes in the form of a newspaper or biographical excerpt, at other times a fictional story. Some readings have been written in narrative format since this encourages pupils to take a more active part.

Reflection: this offers space for thought and a chance to apply the reading to everyday life. In a morning assembly, it presents something for pupils to think about during the day. Whilst the reflections contain many inspiring quotations for silent reflection, they also contain issues for discussion and debate. It is not expected that teachers will use all of the reflections on a topic in any one session. It is for the teacher to choose which is most applicable.

Although all of these stories are for use in school assemblies they are also ideal for small teaching groups – the single class or form group. Many of the readings deal with topics at the heart of personal and social education (PSE) and citizenship education. The book has been written with these two audiences in mind. Many of the assemblies encourage discussion and debate, which could form the heart of a tutor group period.

Introduction

In order for this time of sharing and reflection to work well, a number of points should be kept in mind.

- *Create a more informal seating arrangement in order to encourage a calm and quiet atmosphere. At times consider grouping the pupils around a news-board displaying 'issues of the day' for discussion and evaluation. Music can be used at the beginning of the period to create a break with what has gone before and to make the time together special. Pupils can choose pieces so long as they contribute to creating a meditative atmosphere.*

- *Create a sense of focus. This can be achieved simply – perhaps using a candle or a bowl of flowers. Photographs from newspapers or magazines can also be used on an OHT or a slide.*

- *Pupils should be taught to remain respectful during the readings, although they should also be encouraged to raise relevant questions. It is important that all pupils feel comfortable enough to be able to interact with the material – to provide responses to the questions and reflections.*

- *If this time is to be used to contribute to PSE or citizenship education it will be useful to provide each pupil with an assembly diary, to jot down thoughts, observations and questions as they listen to the reading. It is important that this diary is confidential, so that the pupil can feel free to be honest. This is especially important when pupils are being asked to reflect on themselves – their strengths and weaknesses, their hopes and fears, their virtues and vices and their relationships with others (family, friends and so on). As the class teacher you may like to ask permission to look at these diaries now and then, and to negotiate whether you want to be able to respond to pupil reflections. However, it is important to be clear about the value of your comments and the level of confidentiality to which your pupils are entitled. The teacher is not there to impose his or her values, or even the school's shared values.*

Introduction

Teachers are in the privileged position of being able to act as companions on their pupils' spiritual, moral and cultural journeys. It is hoped that this book will be a useful addition to pack in their bag for the journey.

Part 2

Personal values

1. How to play the game of life

Theme: Acceptance

Introduction

Now and then you meet people who are content and at peace with life. There appears to be nothing that disturbs them. What is the secret of their success? The following reading provides one clue: the ability to accept whatever life offers.

Reading

Nothing surpasses the holiness of those who have learned perfect acceptance of everything that is.

In the game of cards called life one plays the hand one is dealt to the best of one's ability. Those who insist on playing, not the hand they were given, but the one they insist they should have been dealt – these are life's failures.

We are not asked if we will play. That is not an option. Play we must. The option is how.

(*Taking Flight*, Anthony de Mello)

Reflections

- What do you think is meant by 'those who insist on playing, not the hand they were given, but the one they insist they should have been dealt'?

- *Today I will accept what life offers. Today I will learn to celebrate being alive. I try to teach my heart to want nothing it can't have.*

(*The Colour Purple*, Alice Walker)

2. A matter of attitude

Theme: The importance of having a right attitude in life

Introduction

Buddhism teaches that it is important to have a right attitude to life and that each one of us is who we choose to be. The following story illustrates the importance of having the right attitude and comes from the Buddhist tradition.

Reading

Narrator: In Thailand there is a tradition of Buddhist monks travelling from village to village, offering teaching in return for food. One of these monks was called Ananda, which means 'joy' or 'bliss'. Like all Buddhist monks, he owned no possessions of his own – no home and no money. All he had was the saffron robe that clothed him and a beautiful smile that he wore. The smile never left his face. People loved him for his smile, it even made them smile in his presence. One day on his travels Ananda met a young boy.

Boy: Are you a holy man?

Ananda: I am as holy as you are.

Boy: Why don't you own anything?

Ananda: My smile is my own.

Boy: Do you always smile?

Ananda: Yes, even when I am asleep.

Boy: How do you manage always to smile?

Ananda: Smiling is easy. You see I believe in happiness, and I also believe in you.

Narrator: Now both Ananda and the boy were smiling. Ananda knew that in order to be happy a person must believe that happiness is natural to them and everyone else. Ananda chose to be happy.

Reflections

- A happy person is not a person in a certain set of circumstances, but rather a person with a certain set of attitudes.

  (*Happiness Now!*, R. Holden quoting Hugh Down)

- Circumstances and situations do colour life, but you have been given the mind to choose what the colour shall be.

  (*Happiness Now!*, R. Holden quoting John Homer Miller)

- Do you need to make a special effort to enjoy the beauty of the blue sky? Do we have to practise to be able to enjoy it? No, we just enjoy it. Each second, each minute of our lives can be like this. Wherever we are, any time, we have the capacity to enjoy the sunshine, the presence of each other, even the sensation of our breathing. We don't need to go to China to enjoy the blue sky. We don't have to travel into the future to enjoy our breathing. We can be in touch with these things right now.

  (*Present Moment, Wonderful Moment*, Thich Nhat Hanh, Vietnamese Buddhist monk)

3. Decide what you want to be

Theme: Our attitude to life determines what we get out of life

Introduction

We all have within us the ability to be happy or unhappy in life. It's largely a matter of attitude.

Consider where we all come from. When we were babies everything was so exciting to us. The world was brand-new and every day offered us a new discovery. If a newborn baby could talk, he or she would probably say something about what an extraordinary world this is. But as babies grow up the faculty of wonder seems to diminish. The cares of the world take over.

As we grow up we develop certain attitudes. Some people seem always to have a positive mental attitude – they are determined to get the most out of life. However, others seem to be determined to be unhappy as the following stories illustrate.

Reading 1

The Master told his disciples the story of the hotel owner who complained bitterly about the effect on his business of a new highway the government had built.

'Look,' said a friend, 'I just don't understand you. I see a NO VACANCY sign each night in front of your hotel.'

'You can't go by that. Before they built the highway I used to turn away thirty or forty people each day. Now I never turn away more than twenty-five.'

Added the Master, 'When you are determined to feel bad, even non-existent customers are real.'

(*Taking Flight*, Anthony de Mello)

Reading 2

On another occasion a despondent disciple complained that, because of his handicaps, he was being cheated by life.

'Cheated?' cried the Master. 'Cheated? Look around you man! With every moment of consciousness you are being grossly overpaid!'

(*Taking Flight*, Anthony de Mello)

Reflections

- The most common cause of people's unhappiness is the decision they make to be unhappy. It is for this reason that of two people who find themselves in exactly the same situation one will be happy, the other unhappy.

- Decide now what attitude you wish to have.

4. Tetsugen's attempt to print the Buddhist scriptures

Theme: Caring for those in need

Introduction

The religions of the world teach that caring for the poor and needy is one of the holiest things a person can do. Many religions teach that we will be judged at the end of time by the way in which we have, or have not, looked out for those in need.

The following story comes from the Zen Buddhist tradition that became popular in Japan.

Reading

Once upon a time a Zen Buddhist student called Tetsugen set himself the task of printing seven thousand copies of the Buddhist Holy Scriptures. This was a massive work requiring a lot of money. He therefore travelled all over Japan collecting funds for the project.

It took Tetsugen ten years to collect enough money. Although some wealthy people gave him gold coins, most of his money was collected piece by piece from peasants he met along his journey. Just as he was about to invest the money in the printing of the scriptures the River Uji overflowed, leaving thousands of peasants without food and shelter. Tetsugen spent all the money he had collected over the last ten years providing them with enough food and a roof over their heads.

He started his travels again in order to collect funds for his printing project. It was several years before he had collected the required amount. This time, just as he was about to go to print, an epidemic spread across the country. It brought great suffering to many people. Tetsugen did not hesitate to spend all the money he had collected, to relieve the suffering.

For a third time Tetsugen set out across Japan to collect money for the printing of the scriptures. Twenty years after he first started his journeys he finally had enough money to go ahead with his project. His dream had finally come true. The printing block that produced the first edition of the scriptures is today on display at the Obaku Monastery in Kyoto.

To this day the Japanese tell their children that Tetsugen produced three editions of the scriptures in all. They teach that the first two are invisible and are far superior to the third.

Reflections

- The most important distinction between people is between those who love and those who do not show love.

- My humanity is bound up in yours, for we can only be human together.

> (Desmond Tutu, b.1931, South African anti-apartheid activist and religious leader)

- We live very close together. So, our prime purpose in this life is to help others. And if you can't help them at least don't hurt them.

> (Dalai Lama, b.1935, Tibetan spiritual leader)

- How can each one of us do something to show our care for the needy today?

5. The story of Rosa Parks

Theme: Courage to stand up to injustice

Introduction

Courage is the quality shown by someone who decides to do something difficult or dangerous, even though they may be afraid. It is about how you act. It is about mustering the strength to do things you know you should do, even though you may be scared. If you have the 'courage of your convictions', you have the confidence to do what you believe is right, even though other people may disagree with you.

The Greek philosopher, Aristotle (384–322 BCE), observed, 'We become brave by doing brave acts.' What he meant is that we may not feel very brave when we do something which requires courage, but in the act of doing it we become brave and courageous. We overcome our fear.

There are different kinds of courage. In the following story Rosa Parks showed the courage to stand up for what she thought was right. It takes place at the beginning of the civil rights movement in America. This incident was instrumental in bringing about a democratic process by which blacks were granted equal rights to whites.

Reading

It was Thursday, 1 December 1955. The workday was over and crowds of people boarded the green-and-white buses that trundled through the streets of Montgomery. Rosa Parks was tired after a full day of stitching and ironing shirts at the Montgomery Fair department store. She thought she was lucky to have gotten one of the last seats in the rear section of the Cleveland Avenue bus that would take her home.

Soon the back of the bus was full, and several people were standing in the rear. The bus rolled on through Court Square ...

and came to a stop in front of the Empire Theater. The next passenger aboard stood in the front of an aisle. He was a white man.

When he noticed that a white person had to stand, the bus driver, James F. Blake, called out to the four black people who were sitting just behind the white section. He said they would have to give up their seats for the new passenger. No one stood up. 'You'd better make it light on yourself and let me have those seats,' the driver said threateningly. Three men got up and went to stand at the back of the bus. But Rosa Parks wasn't about to move. She had been in this situation before, and she had always given up her seat. She had always felt insulted by the experience. 'It meant that I didn't have a right to do anything but get on the bus, give them my fare, and then be pushed around wherever they wanted me,' she said … She told the driver that she wasn't in the white section and she wasn't going to move.

Blake knew the rules, though. He knew that the white section was wherever the driver said it was. If more white passengers got on the bus, he could stretch the white section to the back of the bus and make all the blacks stand. He shouted to Rosa Parks to move to the back of the bus. She wasn't impressed. She told him again that she wasn't moving. Everyone in the bus was silent, wondering what would happen next. Finally Blake told Rosa Parks that he would have her arrested for violating the racial segregation codes. In a firm but quiet voice, she told him that he could do what he wanted to do because she wasn't moving.

Blake got off the bus and came back with an officer of Montgomery Police Department. As the police officer placed Rosa Parks under arrest, she asked him plainly, 'Why do you people push us around?' With the eyes of all the passengers on him, the officer could only answer in confusion. 'I don't know. I'm just obeying the law,' he said.

Rosa Parks was taken to the police station, where she was booked and fingerprinted … Then a policewoman marched her

Personal values

into a long corridor facing a wall of iron bars. A barred door was slid open. She went inside. The door clanged shut, and she was locked in. She was in jail.

(Rosa Parks's decision to challenge her arrest in court led Montgomery's black community to organize a bus boycott as a show of support.)

Rosa Parks woke up on the morning of Monday December 5, thinking about her trial. As she and her husband got out of bed, they heard the familiar sound of a City Lines bus pulling up to a stop across the road. There was usually a crowd of people waiting for the bus at this time. The Parks's rushed to the window and looked out. Except for the driver, the bus was empty and there was no one getting on either. The bus stood at the stop for more than a minute ... as the puzzled driver waited for passengers. But no one appeared, and the empty bus chugged away.

Rosa Parks was filled with happiness. Her neighbours were actually boycotting the buses. She couldn't wait to drive to the courthouse so that she could see how the boycott was going in the rest of Montgomery ... All over the city, empty buses bounced around for everyone to see. There was never more than the usual small group of white passengers in front and sometimes a lonely black passenger in back, wondering what was going on. The streets were filled with black people walking to work.

As Rosa Parks and her lawyer drove up to the courthouse, there was another surprise waiting for them. A crowd of about five hundred blacks had gathered to show their support for her. Mrs Parks and the lawyer made their way slowly through the cheering crowd into the courtroom. Once they were inside, the trial didn't take long. Rosa Parks was quickly convicted of breaking the bus segregation laws and fined ten dollars, as well as four dollars for the cost of her trial ... This time, however, Fred Gray (her lawyer) rose to file an appeal on Rosa Parks's case. This meant that her case would be taken to a higher court at a later date. Meanwhile, Mrs Parks was free to go.

Outside the courthouse, the crowd was getting restless. Some of them were carrying sawn-off shotguns, and the policemen were beginning to look worried … Voices from the crowd shouted out that they would storm the courthouse if Rosa Parks didn't come out safely within a few minutes. When she did appear, a great cheer went up.

After seeing the empty buses that morning, and this large and fearless crowd around her now, Rosa Parks knew that she had made the right decision. Black people were uniting to show the city administration that they were tired of the insults of segregation. Together, they could change Montgomery. They could do some good.

(*Rosa Parks: The Movement Organizes*, Kai Friese)

Reflections

- Is there anything you would be willing to stand up for, even if it meant that you might go to jail for it?

- Are there times when you should disobey the law in order to stand up for what is right?

- *Without courage, you cannot practise any other virtue. You have to have courage – courage of different kinds: first intellectual courage, to sort out different values and make up your mind. You have to have moral courage to stick up to that – no matter what comes in your way, no matter what the obstacle and the opposition is. Opposition comes not only from your enemies but sometimes from your friends, and the latter is much more difficult to face. You have to have physical courage, because very often going along the path of your choice is full of physical hardship.*

(Indira Gandhi, 1917–1984, Indian Prime Minister)

Personal values

- *You gain strength, courage and confidence by every experience by which you really stop to look fear in the face. You are able to say to yourself, 'I lived through this horror. I can take the next thing that comes along.'*

  (Eleanor Roosevelt, 1884–1962, American humanitarian and wife of the US President

6. Menashe and the rabbi's letter

Theme: Character: the struggle to act with integrity

Introduction

A person's character takes a long time to establish, but it is easy to break. In the following story a good man did one thing out of character and thereby lost his integrity and gave away his good name. In giving away his good name it was as if he ceased to exist.

Reading

The Israeli writer S.Y. Agnon tells the story of a simple but decent man named Menashe. He owned a grocery stall but this collapsed due to his kindness and generosity. Menashe could not bear to ask for money from people who could not afford to pay. Menashe's ruthless competitors brought an end to his business. He had no alternative but to close the shop and to go from town to town begging. The rabbi of his village gave him a letter testifying to the fact that he was a good man who deserved to be helped.

Menashe spent a year travelling from village to village collecting charity. With the help of the rabbi's letter he collected enough to be able to go back to his own town and start another business. On the last night before he returned he stayed at an inn. At the same inn there was a thief who saw Menashe's letter. 'With a letter like that I could do very well.' He offered Menashe a large sum of money in exchange for the letter which, after all, he no longer needed.

Menashe was tempted. He sold the letter and went into town to celebrate. He now had more money than he had ever had. In town he got drunk and was robbed of everything. Lacking the money even to travel home he started begging all over again.

Personal values

Meanwhile the thief was himself robbed by a highwayman and left in the gutter to die. When his body was found, with Menashe's letter in his pocket, news was sent back home that Menashe was dead. The rabbi declared that his wife was free to remarry. Several months later she remarried, and a year later gave birth to a son.

The real Menashe painfully worked his way home. On arriving in his village he saw his wife with her new husband. What should he do? If he declared himself alive his wife would be found to be an adulteress, and her child branded illegitimate. He couldn't do that to someone he loved. And so he decided to live on the outskirts of the town in the cemetery. He told his sad story to the man who cared for the cemetery. Soon Menashe died and the custodian buried him by the stone his wife had set up for him two years earlier.

Reflections

- By selling the letter Menashe was acting out of character. He was trying to make a quick profit. By doing so he compromised his integrity and this became his downfall. It was only when he returned to his village and protected the reputation of his wife and her son that he re-established himself as a man of decency and integrity.

- When we do something wrong we lose our integrity. Being human means that we are not going to be perfect, but it also means that we should always be struggling to do the good thing, to act out of our wholeness and integrity.

7. Compassion in action

Theme: Practising the skill of empathy

Introduction

Empathy is the ability to know how another person feels, to share their feelings and emotions as if they were your own. The ability to empathize builds on your ability to know yourself. The more open you are to your own emotions, the more skilled you will be in reading the feelings of others.

The ability to empathize with somebody is a very important skill in life. It comes into play in relationships with boyfriends, girlfriends and partners, in businesses such as sales and management, and in the ability to be compassionate to those in need throughout the world.

One of the most famous lines in literature, 'Never send to know for whom the bell tolls; it tolls for thee' was written by John Donne. He was drawing attention to the link between empathy and caring: another's pain is one's own. The following reading tells the story of one person who practised this ability to empathize with others – to feel their joys and pains.

Reading

Princess Diana has been remembered for her ability to reach out to others, to show empathy and care.

In the weeks after her tragic death thousands of people brought floral tributes to Kensington Palace, addressed to 'The Queen of Hearts'. Overnight it became clear that Diana had captured the hearts of ordinary people all over the world. She had become an icon of human compassion.

Diana was unafraid of showing emotion, her own weakness and vulnerability. She used her ability to empathize to reach out to others in their need. She did not hide her unhappy childhood, nor her struggles with bulimia and the breakdown of her

Personal values

marriage. Instead, she allowed people to identify with her all too human struggles. She had the human touch – the ability to reach out to others and show that she cared.

Reflections

- *Great opportunities to help others seldom come, but small ones surround us every day.*
  (Sally Koch in *Chicken Soup for the Teenage Soul*)

- The root of caring is the ability to empathize – to feel another's pain and joy. Make room in your mind for others. Now and then we all need to reshuffle the furniture in our mind: to clear out all our stuff to make room for others.

8. How much land does a person need?

Theme: Learning to be content

Introduction

Have you ever heard the saying, 'The grass is always greener on the other side'? It is easy to feel that other people's lives are far better than our own and to start to feel discontent with our lot. However, we should choose carefully what we strive for, as the following story shows.

Reading

The great Russian novelist Leo Tolstoy tells the story of two sisters who were married, one to a rich merchant in the town, the other to a poor peasant in the countryside. One day the poor sister visited her rich elder sister, who started to boast of all their luxury and the advantages of living in the town. The younger sister felt attacked and replied, 'I would not change my life: we may not have all your riches but we are content. We may not be rich but we have enough to eat.'

Pahom, the peasant, listened attentively to the two sisters. He started to think, 'True we have enough to eat, but only just. We have to work from sun-break to sunset in order to make enough food. Our trouble is that we haven't enough land. If I had enough property I shouldn't fear the Devil himself.'

The Devil was listening to the whole conversation and was secretly pleased that the peasant's wife had led her husband into wishing for more land, so much that he would not fear the Devil himself. 'All right. I shall give him plenty of land, but we shall see if he does not fall into my power.'

Close to the peasant's village there lived a small landowner. The news got around that she was about to sell her property. Pahom approached the lady himself. He had one hundred rubles put aside. He sold a colt and hired out their sons as labourers. Eventually they had enough money to buy twenty acres straight out. So now Pahom had land of his own. He borrowed seed and sowed it on the land he had bought. The harvest was a good one and he managed to pay off all his debts in the first year.

So Pahom was very contented, that is until one day a peasant from beyond the Volga was passing through the village. He stayed the night with Pahom and his wife, and over supper told them of his hometown where the land was so good that crops were larger than anywhere else. Furthermore, each person settling on the land was given 25 acres for free. Pahom could not resist. 'Why should I live here where I have to work so hard when I could live in a better land where the crops are so bountiful?'

And so towards summer Pahom started out. When he reached the place the stranger had talked about he saw that it was just as he said – lush and plentiful. He returned home, sold his land for a profit and moved his family to their new piece of land. He was ten times better off than he had been. At first he was extremely contented. This is all he could have wished for. But after some years Pahom started to grow restless. He started to feel that even here he hadn't enough land.

A passing dealer happened to stop at Pahom's one day and they had a talk. He said that he was just returning from the land of the Bashkirs, far away, where he had bought thirteen thousand acres of land, all for 1000 rubles. Pahom questioned him further and the dealer told him, 'All you need to do is to make friends with the Chiefs.' Pahom inquired how to get to the place and, as soon as the dealer went on his way, Pahom left his wife and set out for the land of the Bashkirs.

On the way he stopped at a town to buy presents to give to the Chiefs. After seven days he eventually arrived at the land he had been told about. It was indeed the most beautiful land he had ever seen. As soon as the Chiefs saw Pahom they came out of their tents. He talked with them and distributed his gifts. Pahom talked about his desire to buy land from them. 'You can have as much land as you wish – we have as much as the eye can see and more.' 'And what will be the price?' asked Pahom. 'Our price is always the same,' replied the Chief. 'One thousand rubles a day.' Pahom did not understand. 'A day – what sort of measurement is that?' 'We do not know how to reckon it out,' said the Chief. 'We sell it by the day. As much land as you can walk around in a day is yours for the price.'

Pahom couldn't believe what he was hearing. Beautiful arable land stretched out in front of him as far as his eyes could see. You could walk a long way in a day. The Chief laughed when he looked at Pahom, and warned him, 'It will all be yours. But there is one condition. If you don't return on the same day you lose the land and we keep your money.'

Pahom was delighted. They agreed a deal for the next day. Pahom lay awake all night and dozed off just before dawn. Hardly were his eyes closed when he had a dream. He thought he heard someone laughing outside his tent. When he went to look he found it was the Bashkir Chief. Going nearer to the Chief, Pahom asked, 'What are you laughing at?' But he saw that it was no longer the Chief, but the dealer who had stopped at his house. Just as he was about to ask, 'Have you been here long?' he saw that it was not the dealer but the peasant who had come from up the Volga. Then he saw that it was not the peasant either but the Devil himself sitting there and chuckling. Before the Devil lay a man, barefoot, face on the ground. When Pahom looked carefully he saw that the man was dead and it was himself! Pahom awoke horror-struck.

Pahom rose from his bed in beads of sweat. Together with the Chief they made their way to the top of a hill overlooking the pastures. The Chief took off his fox-fur cap and laid it on the ground. Pahom put his money in it. 'This will be the point. Start from here and return to here before sunset.'

Personal values

Pahom started out in the direction of the rising sun. He walked all day using turf as markers to the boundary of his property. By late afternoon the sun was extremely hot and so he took off his shoes and coat. The hill could scarcely be seen. He realized that time was running out. He was still ten miles from his goal. He was now walking with difficulty. His bare feet were cut and bruised and his legs began to fail. He longed to rest but could not. The sun was starting to descend in the sky.

'Oh dear,' he thought. 'I could lose everything for trying to go too far.' He started to run, but he was still far from his goal and the sun was falling quickly. 'What shall I do,' he thought again. 'I have grasped too much and ruined the whole affair.' This fear made him all the more anxious. Though afraid that he might die he dare not stop. The sun was close to the rim as he heard the shouts of the Bashkirs jeering him on.

Pahom could see the fox-cap as he pushed himself up the hill. He also saw the Chief holding his sides and laughing. He remembered his dream. 'There is plenty of land,' he thought, 'but will God let me live to see it?' With all his remaining strength he forced himself to the top just as the sky went dark. He collapsed at the feet of the Chief, completely exhausted. 'Ah, that's a fine fellow,' exclaimed the Chief. He had gained much land. Pahom's servant ran to his master, but as he approached he saw blood trickle from his mouth. Pahom was dead!

(adapted from *Walk in the Light and twenty three tales*, Leo Tolstoy)

Reflections

- What is life about? Is it about striving for more and more riches and possessions?

- *If you become very rich, even become a millionaire or a billionaire, on the day of your death, no matter how much money you have in the bank, there isn't any little piece of it*

that you can take with you. The death of a rich person and the death of a wild animal, each is just the same.
(*Ocean of Wisdom: Guidelines for Living*, Dalai Lama)

- *Wealth and fame are of dubious value when we think that life is like a fleeting dream.*
(*Ching-hua yuan, Flowers in the Mirror*, Li Ju-chen, c.1763–1830)

9. To forgive or not to forgive?

Theme: Our ability to forgive others

Introduction

Why do we find it so hard to say sorry when we have done things wrong? Why do we harbour grudges against other people? Wouldn't it be so much easier to forgive others and ourselves?

The following reading is taken from a Jewish liturgy which is said at Yom Kippur, that time in the Jewish year when people ask forgiveness from God, and from neighbours they have hurt. This is the prayer which President Clinton read in his famous 'Prayer Breakfast Apology' for the Lewinsky affair.

Reading

Now is the time for turning

The leaves are beginning to turn from green to red to orange

The birds are beginning to turn and are heading once more toward the south

The animals are beginning to turn to storing their food for the winter

For leaves, birds and animals, turning comes instinctively

But for us, turning does not come so easily

It takes an act of will for us to make a turn. It means breaking old habits.

It means admitting that we have been wrong, and this is never easy.

It means losing face. It means starting all over again. And this is always painful. It means saying I am sorry.

It means recognizing that we have the ability to change. These things are terribly hard to do.

But unless we turn, we will be trapped for ever in yesterday's ways.

Lord help us to turn from callousness to sensitivity, from hostility to love, from pettiness to purpose, from envy to contentment, from carelessness to discipline, from fear to faith.

Turn us around, oh, Lord, and bring us back toward you. Revive our lives as at the beginning.

And turn us toward each other, Lord, for in isolation, there is no life.

(*Gates of Repentance*, Shaarei Teshuva)

Reflections

- Why doesn't turning come easily to some of us?

- What does each of us need to turn from today? Resolve to give up your grudges and be willing to start again.

- The more we know the better we forgive.

- *Whoever feels deeply, feels for all who live.*
  (Madame de Stael in *Chicken Soup for the Teenage Soul*)

10. The old woman and her visions

Theme: Learning to forgive ourselves as we forgive others

Introduction

Have you done anything for which you find it hard to forgive yourself? Sometimes people find it easier to forgive others than to forgive themselves.

Reading

There was an old woman living in the village who became famous for the visions she was receiving from God. The priest wanted to test whether these visions were really true and so he set a little test for her. 'When God next appears to you in a vision ask him to tell you my sins. Only He and I know them. That should be proof enough that your visions are real.'

After a month the priest called on the old lady and asked her if she'd received any more visions. 'Yes,' she replied. 'Did you ask God to tell you my sins?' 'Indeed, I did.' 'What was his answer?' the priest asked, with a certain nervousness in his voice.

'He said, "Tell your priest I have forgotten his sins."'

Reflections

- Learn to ask forgiveness from others and then to forgive yourself. Forgiveness leads to healing.

- There is a saying, 'To know all is to forgive all'. All of us do things wrong at times. No one is perfect enough to judge other people. We should learn to forgive others and also ourselves on a daily basis.

11. Damon and Pythias

Theme: Friendship is based upon trust and self-sacrifice

Introduction

What qualities make up a good friendship? Friendship is more than just hanging around with someone and sharing a joke. The Greek philosopher Aristotle said, 'We may describe friendly feeling towards any one as wishing for him what you believe to be good things, not for your own sake but for his, and being inclined, so far as you can, to bring these things about.'

True friendship has a selfless quality about it. A true friend is willing to sacrifice his or her own interests in order to help another. True friendship is based on a deep trust between people. It can be a risky business as the following story illustrates.

Reading

Damon and Pythias had been best friends since early childhood. They trusted each other like brothers and knew from early on that they were willing to lay down their lives for each other if it came to it. One day their friendship was put to the test. It happened this way.

Pythias was a brave young scholar who always spoke the truth, even when it would have been wiser to remain silent. Dionysius, the ruler of Syracuse, grew annoyed when he heard that Pythias was teaching that no one man should have absolute power over others. He summoned him to his palace and asked him what trouble he was trying to stir up. 'Why are you spreading unrest amongst the people?' Pythias replied, 'I only tell the truth.' At this Dionysius became enraged at such an attack on his authority. 'Retract, or else I shall have you killed.' 'I will retract nothing,' Pythias replied. 'Then you will die,' said Dionysius. 'Do you have any last requests?' 'I wish only one thing – to

Personal values

return to my home to say goodbye to my wife and children. Then I shall return to you and you may have your will.'

'Do you think I am stupid as well as unjust?' the ruler replied. At this point Damon came to the support of his friend. 'Sir, trust him. I will stay here as your prisoner until Pythias returns. Our friendship is well known to you. You can be sure Pythias will return so long as you hold me.' 'Very well, if Pythias does not return you will die in his place.' 'He will keep his word,' Damon replied.

After several days when Pythias failed to reappear the ruler began to taunt Damon. 'Your time is almost up. Your friend will never return. You were a fool to rely upon him.' 'He has merely been delayed,' Damon answered. 'The winds have been against him. I am confident that my friend will return soon.' Finally Dionysius lost his patience. He summoned the executioner to bring Damon to the scaffold. He would take the place of his trouble-making friend. Damon was led from the prison to the executioner. Dionysius greeted him with a smile. 'Your friend has deserted you. What on earth made you trust him? Did you really think that he would sacrifice his own life?' 'He is my friend,' Damon answered. 'I trust him.'

At this the doors flung open and Pythias stumbled in. His back was cut with whips. His face looked drained of all blood. 'Dear Damon, I have only just made it in time. I was kidnapped on my way back and beaten to near death. Thank goodness that I have made it in time.' At this Dionysius was astonished at such a show of loyalty. He revoked his sentence. 'I never believed that such friendship existed – such trust and loyalty. Teach me how to be worthy of such friendship.'

Reflections

- What would you be willing to do for your friends?

- Aristotle said that friends look out for the good of each other. What might this mean? Does it sometimes mean speaking honestly with a friend, even when it might hurt?

- How far should anyone remain loyal to a friend?

12. Friendship

Theme: The nature of true friendship

Introduction

Choose your friends wisely because they say a lot about you. The type of people you hang around with says something about the qualities that you value in others. Good friends help lift you up. Bad friends pull you down. Good friends bring out the best in you. Bad friends may tempt you into trouble.

The following reading illustrates how our ideas on friendship develop as we grow and change.

Reading

In your first year of school your idea of a good friend was the person who let you have the red crayon when all that was left was the ugly black one.

In Year 2 your idea of a good friend was the person who went to the bathroom with you and held your hand as you walked through the scary halls.

In Year 3 your idea of a good friend was the person who helped you stand up to the class bully.

In Year 4 your idea of a good friend was the person who shared their lunch with you when you forgot yours on the bus.

In Year 5 your idea of a good friend was the person who was willing to switch partners in gym so you wouldn't have to be stuck with Nasty Nicky or Smelly Susan.

In Year 6 your idea of a friend was the person who saved a seat in the back of the bus for you.

In Year 7 your idea of a friend was the person who went up to Nick or Susan, your new crush, and asked them to dance with you, so that if they said no you wouldn't have to be embarrassed.

In Year 8 your idea of a friend was the person who let you copy the history homework that you had forgotten about, from the night before.

In Year 9 your idea of a good friend was the person who helped you pack up your stuffed animals and old childish toys so that your room would be a teenager's room, but didn't laugh at you when you finished and broke down in tears.

In Year 10 your idea of a good friend was the person who went with you to that 'cool' party thrown by a sixthformer so you wouldn't be the only one there who was in Year 10.

In Year 11 your idea of a good friend was the person who changed their schedule so you would have someone to sit with at lunch.

In Year 12 your idea of a good friend was the person who gave you rides in their new car, convinced your parents that you shouldn't be grounded, consoled you when you broke up with Nick or Susan, and found you a date to the end-of-year party.

In Year 13 your idea of a good friend was the person who helped you pick out a college, assured you that you would get into that college, and helped you deal with your parents who were having a hard time adjusting to the idea of letting you go.

The summer after Year 13 your idea of a good friend was the person who helped you clean up the bottles from that party, helped you sneak out of the house when you just couldn't deal with your parents. They assured you that now that you and Nick or you and Susan were back together, you could make it through anything. They helped you pack up for college and just silently hugged you as you looked through blurry eyes at eighteen years

Personal values

of memories you were leaving behind. And finally, on those last days of childhood, they went out of their way to come over and send you off with a hug and – most importantly – with the knowledge that you were loved.

Now, your idea of a good friend is still the person who gives you the better of the two choices, holds your hand when you're scared, and helps you fight off those who try to take advantage of you. They go out of their way to make time for you, and help you deal with pressure from others. They smile for you when they are sad, and help you become a better person. Most importantly, they love you.

Reflections

- Simply saying you are friends doesn't make it so. True friends look out for each other, especially when things get tough. Friends go out of their way for each other and protect each others' interests.

- Some people come into our lives and go just as quickly. Some stay for a while and leave footprints on our hearts. And we are never, ever the same.

- Take care of yourself and each other!

13. The precious book

Theme: Generosity of spirit

Introduction

Do you think you are a generous person? Generosity is not just about giving things away, it is also about how you feel and how you treat other people. A person who is generous in their conduct and feelings towards others is called magnanimous. In the following story an abbot shows magnanimity to a fellow monk.

Reading

In medieval times monasteries were centres of great learning. You may have seen the film *The Name of the Rose*, where the library was based upon an old monastery library in Austria.

In the heart of Germany, Abbot Seraphim looked after one of the best libraries of the time. The books were made of very fine parchment and worth a lot of money. One particular book, a commentary on the monastic rule, was especially precious. One day a visiting monk saw the precious book and slipped it into his bag when he left. Abbot Seraphim soon noticed that the book was missing and knew exactly who had taken it.

The monk went into the city to attempt to sell the book. He entered the largest bookstore and asked if the manager was interested in buying it. He was asking five pounds for it. That was a lot of money in those days. The manager looked over the book and asked to keep it for two days so that he could examine it.

After two days the monk returned to the bookseller. The buyer told the monk that he had consulted with Abbot Seraphim up at the monastery on the top of the hill. All of the blood drained out of the monk's face. 'What did Abbot Seraphim tell you?' he

Personal values

asked the buyer. 'He said that at five pounds the book was a bargain and that I should buy it,' replied the manager.

'Didn't he say anything else?' asked the frightened monk. 'No, nothing at all.' At that the monk apologized for wasting the manager's time and said that the book was no longer for sale. He quickly made his way up to the monastery and banged on the door, demanding to see Abbot Seraphim. When he was let into his room he fell on his knees begging the Abbot for forgiveness. The Abbot gently replied, 'The book is my present to you.' However, the monk replied, 'If you do not take the book back I will have no peace.'

From that point on the monk stayed with the Abbot.

Reflections

- In what way did Abbot Seraphim demonstrate generosity of spirit?

- Do you think the Abbot did the right thing? Is it practical to act in a magnanimous way today? For example, think about a similar incident of shoplifting.

14. A great man died today

Theme: Appreciating goodness

Introduction

What makes a person great? What qualities do they possess? I guess you could call the following man a truly great person, and yet most people on this earth never knew him.

The following reading was written the night after this great man's death.

Reading

A great man died today. He wasn't a leader of a nation nor a famous war hero or sportsman. He never made a million on the stock market, nor did you ever see his name in the papers. But he was one of the greatest men I have ever known. He was my father.

He never went to university and gained a degree. In fact he finished school at sixteen and, as far as I am aware, never received any honours or credits throughout his life. He did corny things like paying his bills on time, declaring the correct amount on his tax form, going to church on Sunday and looking after his parents as they reached old age. He encouraged his children to do their best, always pushing them to fulfil their potential but never setting unrealistic expectations. He was proud of his family and showed patience with his wife, especially after she suffered a number of strokes.

Tonight is my first night without him. I don't know what to do with myself. I am sorry now for the times when I didn't truly appreciate my dad, when I took him for granted. But I am grateful for a lot of other things.

Personal values

I am grateful for the way he never spoke down to people – the way he treated them all as equals, be they people with authority or the homeless. Of all the gifts he has left me, the most important is his conviction that there is never a need to insult another person, that each person has a sacredness about them. That wonderful man died with a smile on his face and contentment in his heart. He knew that he was a great success as a father and husband. I wonder how many millionaires can say that?

Reflections

• What is true greatness?

• What are the great things that you would like to remembered for?

• Who are the people you admire in life? Learn to appreciate them now.

15. The good bishop

Theme: Honesty

Introduction

Early on in life you will be judged as an honest or dishonest person. When people know that you are honest you will be trusted and liked. Dishonest people are distrusted. It is easy to gain a reputation early on in life and hard to change a reputation once it is gained.

Les Miserables is one of the most popular musicals today. It tells the story of Jean Valjean, a man who had gained a reputation for being dishonest but who was then transformed into a honest man by the power of forgiveness.

Reading

Jean Valjean was a wood-chopper's son who was left as a orphan when he was very young. His elder sister, who by that time had married, brought him up. However, when he was just seventeen years old his sister's husband died and he was left to bring up her seven little children. Wood chopping paid a poor salary, and he found it very difficult to find enough money to feed the family.

One winter's day Jean was without work. The children were crying from hunger. Desperately he went out in the middle of the night and broke into a bakery to steal bread for the children. The next morning he was arrested and sent to prison. During his years in prison he became a hardened man, feared by the other inmates. Eventually Valjean earned his release.

Convicts in those days had to carry identity cards and no innkeeper would let a dangerous prisoner spend the night under his roof. For four days he wandered the village roads, seeking shelter against the weather, until finally a kindly bishop had mercy on him. That night Jean Valjean lay still until the bishop

Personal values

drifted off to sleep. Then he rose from his bed, stole the family silver and crept off into the darkness.

The next morning three policemen knocked on the bishop's door. They had Valjean with them. They had caught the convict as he fled with the silver and were ready to put the thief in chains for life. However, the bishop responded in a way that no one, especially Jean Valjean, expected. 'So here you are! I'm delighted to see you. Have you forgotten that I gave you the candlesticks as well? They're silver like the rest, and worth a good 200 francs. Did you forget to take them?'

Jean Valjean was now staring at the bishop, unable to believe what he had just heard. The bishop turned to the police. 'Valjean is no thief. This silver was my gift to him.' When the police withdrew, the bishop gave the candlesticks to his guest, now speechless and trembling. 'Do not forget, do not ever forget that you have promised me to use the money to make yourself an honest man.'

The power of the bishop's act changed Jean Valjean's life. He felt forgiven, even though he had never asked for it. He kept the candlesticks as a precious memory and dedicated himself from then on to helping others in need. However, this is not the end of the story.

In the original novel there is a detective named Javert who is angered by the forgiveness that the bishop shows Valjean. He stalks Valjean over the next two decades. Javert is consumed by a desire for retribution. Then, after Valjean saves Javert's life, the detective senses his black-and-white world beginning to crumble. Unable to cope with such an act Javert jumps off a bridge into the River Seine.

Reflections

- In what ways did Valjean change as a result of his encounter with the bishop? How was the bishop different from the detective Javert?

- In what sense was Javert's world 'black and white'? What do people mean when they use this phrase? Do you think that life is black and white?

- What reputation do you think you have in life?

- Do you think it is easy to change a reputation once you have gained it? If you had a poor reputation in people's eyes what could you do to change it?

16. The emperor learns an important lesson

Theme: Honesty is the best policy

Introduction

The following story comes from Mexico. It reminds us of the power of an honest act to inspire others.

Reading

During the time of the Aztecs, an emperor ruled who liked to take off his royal robes, disguise himself as a lowly peasant and walk the city streets of his kingdom. He knew that his subjects would speak more honestly to him when he was dressed as a peasant than they would if he appeared as the emperor.

One day, during one of his walks, he came upon a peasant boy gathering sticks to make a fire for his family. It was a hot day and the boy was sweating under the work. He had only managed to gather a small handful, hardly enough to keep a fire alight for even one hour. 'There's hardly enough wood here to light a fire,' said the emperor to the peasant boy. 'Why don't you climb that hill and gather the wood from the forest at the top?' The boy replied, 'I cannot – that wood belongs to the emperor. No one is permitted to take wood from his forest.'

The emperor replied, 'But look at all the wood up there. Surely the emperor must be selfish to make such a rule when his subjects are in such need.' 'It is true that the law is unjust,' replied the peasant boy, 'but there must be another way of getting wood other than breaking the emperor's laws.' The young boy picked up his small pile of sticks and headed for home.

The next day a royal messenger visited the peasant boy and his family at home. The boy and his family were commanded to appear at the palace. The emperor wanted to see them. They put on their best clothes and fearfully made their way to the palace at the top of the hill. They were led in to see the emperor. The peasant boy recognized him at once and was terrified.

'Don't be afraid. You have done no wrong. You refused to disobey my commands. Your parents have raised you well. I sent for them because I wanted to reward them.' With that, the emperor pointed to a chest of gold. There were enough coins there to keep the boy and his family comfortably for the rest of their days.

'There is something more important,' the emperor went on. 'You have taught me that my law is unjust. From now on the royal wood is open to all.' He took the boy by his arm and told him, 'You wondered whether there must be another way. There is – your honesty has reached the heart of the emperor.'

Reflections

- A person's reputation is built upon honest acts. It is important to act in an honest way even when no one is there to notice.

- *Let the world know you as you are, not as you think you should be, because sooner or later, if you are posing, you will forget the pose, and then where are you?*
  (Fanny Brice, 1891–1951, American comedian and singer)

17. The life and work of Paul Cezanne (1839–1906)

Theme: Humility in greatness

Introduction

Today we often hear people boasting about their achievements. They want people to know how rich they are, or how important their job is. However, some of the greatest people in the world have been those with the virtue of humility. The following reading tells the story of one of the most famous painters of the nineteenth century, who embodied the virtue of humility.

Reading

For the first thirty-five years of his life as a painter the great French artist, Paul Cezanne, went unnoticed by the artistic world. He produced masterpieces which he gave away to his neighbours as gifts. He loved his work so much that he never thought about becoming rich and famous because of his art. He certainly didn't presume to think that he would one day be known as the father of modern painting.

He became famous through an art dealer from Paris who saw his paintings and offered to hold an exhibition in his honour. His first one-man exhibition took place in November 1895. It was a great success. The world recognized that he was a great artist. Cezanne was equally surprised by his own fame.

He arrived at the art gallery, supported on the arm of his son. He was amazed when he saw his own paintings, all framed and hanging in a gallery. Turning to his son he said, 'Look, they have framed them!'

Of all the artists which lived at this time Cezanne has perhaps had the most profound effect on art in the twentieth century. Through his landscape paintings he taught people to see the world in a new way. Unlike many people of his day, he was not interested in merely reproducing the world in his paintings. Instead, he was interested in showing what emotions the landscape evoked in him, and thereby was formative in the founding of the so-called abstract art of the twentieth century.

Reflections

- Music needs the hollowness of a clarinet. Writing needs the blankness of the page. Lights needs the openness of the window. Humility needs the absence of the self.

- Do a kind deed for somebody today without anyone knowing that you have done it. Practise humility. Listen to others before you tell them about yourself. Be available for others.

- *Whoever humbles himself, God elevates him; whoever is proud, God brings him down. Whoever runs after honors, honors run away from him.*
  (Talmud, c.late fourth–early sixth century, ancient body of Jewish civil and canonical law, Erubin 13)

- *Those who boast are seldom the great.*
  (Jawaharial Nehru, 1889–1964, Indian Prime Minister)

18. Archbishop Basil Hume

Theme: Humility

Introduction

A humble person is someone who is not puffed up with their own importance. They do not boast or promote themselves. It is a rare but precious quality to find in a person.

Sextus, a Greek philosopher, instructed people to speak 'in few and sensible words, without clamour: a wise person is known by the fewness of their words.' Wise people are often humble. Today's reading tells the story of one such person – the late Roman Catholic Archbishop, Basil Hume.

Reading

On Saturday 26 June 1999, thousands of people from all over the world came together to mourn the death of a much-loved man, Archbishop Basil Hume. Each came with their own sense of personal loss. In a quite extraordinary way it seemed that everyone there thought of him as their personal friend.

In one sense it was odd that such a man should attract such a vast audience. Back in 1975, when he was being considered for the highest post in the Roman Catholic Church in Britain, a newspaper stated that the main disadvantage of this man was he was 'Much too humble to make known his abilities. Could easily be missed!' Twenty-three years later, it was his humility that drew so many to him. He liked to be addressed as 'Father Basil' rather than 'Your Eminence'. He seldom wore his bishop's cross, preferring the robes of a simple monk.

Throughout his life Basil Hume was more fearful of praise than criticism. He became known as a man of deep personal holiness. When people were in his presence they felt that they were close to glimpsing the nature of God. Here was a monk and an archbishop who touched the lives of people deep down, because he knew and loved God.

Throughout his life his heart was touched by the plight of the poor. This great love grew from a belief that each person is made in the image of God and is uniquely loved and valued by God. Basil Hume was moved by the pitiful state of so many homeless people in London that in winter he opened up the cathedral for them to sleep in, and set up the Cardinal Hume Centre for young people at risk.

Basil Hume learnt he had cancer just two months before he died. And how did he prepare himself for his death? The pattern of his final days showed he was almost totally at peace with what he termed his 'new future'. In those final weeks the Cardinal's one prayer was, 'Father, into your hands I commend my spirit.' All of his life he saw himself as the pilgrim on a journey towards God.

Reflections

- *The more you forget yourself, the more Jesus will think of you.*
  (*Life in the Spirit*, Mother Teresa)

- *Hide the good you do, and make known the good done to you.*
  (Ali, c.600–661, first Imam of the Sh'iah branch of Islam, fourth caliph)

- *Hide your good deeds as well as your evil ones.*
  (Bishr al Hafifi, 767–842, Persian Sufi ascetic)

19. A simple act of kindness

Theme: Kindness

Introduction

The following true story illustrates the truth that a simple act of kindness can bring about great happiness.

Reading

We were on holiday. It was a beautiful summer's day – an ideal time for sightseeing. Having spent the morning visiting a quaint little village in the hills we decided to pick up a quick snack for lunch before heading for the beach.

When my friend Sally headed for a hot dog stand I chose to keep her company. The owner put together the perfect hot dog, a juicy sausage topped with ketchup and mustard. When Sally went to pay, the vendor refused her money. The man surprised us. 'It was cooked a few minutes ago and has gone a little cool, so never mind paying me. It will be my freebie for the day.'

We said our thanks and went to sit on the bench on the promenade. As we ate and talked, a man sitting on the next bench distracted me. He was obviously homeless – dressed in rough clothes. As Sally finished off her hot dog she went to put the papers in the bin. 'Any food left in it?' the man from the other bench asked. 'No, it's completely gone,' Sally replied.

'Oh,' was his only reply. He didn't say it in a gruff or annoyed way. He was obviously used to asking the question many times. He was hungry and couldn't bear to see anything thrown away. I felt bad about the man but didn't know what I should do. That's when Sally said, 'Stay right here. I'll be back in a minute.' At which point she went over to the hot dog stand and bought another hot dog. She went and gave it to the man on the other bench.

When she came back to me she said, 'I was just passing on the kindness that the vendor gave to me.' That day I learned how generosity can pass from one person to the next. By giving you teach others how to give.

Reflections

- *Be kind, for everyone you meet is fighting a harder battle.*
  (Plato c.428–347 BCE, Greek philosopher)

- Practise being generous today. Pass on kindness to someone who needs it – it can be in giving a smile, or saying hello, or showing a practical kindness.

- Henry James's nephew once asked the great novelist what he ought to do with his life. He received this advice: three things in human life are important – the first is to be kind; the second is to be kind; and the third is to be kind.

20. A random act of kindness

Theme: Kindness

Introduction

How do you react to people who are rude to you? Do you ever think for a moment what is making them rude – perhaps something going wrong in their life – or do you feel the need to react badly to them?

The following story is an everyday event but it shows that small acts of kindness can transform people's lives, bringing a ray of hope into an otherwise dark world.

Reading

Four years ago the washing machine broke. A very bad-tempered man turned up to mend it. He found it virtually impossible to be polite. I decided that it was best to leave him to mend the machine by himself. When he had finished he had to wait for his colleague to come and take away the old drum. I offered him a cup of coffee. He refused. He didn't seem to want to enter into conversation. Instead, he sat silently at the kitchen table.

After a few minutes he asked about my solar-powered pager which was lying on a workbench. It was an up-to-date model with a good memory inside to record messages. I explained how it worked. He said nothing, but I noticed that he kept looking at it.

After about twenty minutes his assistant came. They took the broken parts down to the van and he returned with the bill for my signature. He turned to leave. Suddenly I asked him to wait a minute. I went and got hold of the pager and gave it to him. 'Are you serious?' he asked. I said yes and smiled. He nodded and started to leave. He hesitated, then turned back and said, 'My wife left me four weeks ago, and this is the first nice thing anyone's done for me.' He looked at me for another moment and left.

I walked back to the kitchen and broke down in tears.

Reflections

- Why did the woman in the story start crying when the man left?

- We all want to feel appreciated by others. As pupils we want to feel that we are appreciated and respected by teachers. Teachers also want to feel appreciated by pupils. The same is true of our family relationships. What can you do today to show your appreciation towards someone?

21. Looking after each other

Theme: Showing kindness

Introduction

You never can tell what type of impact you may make on someone else's life by your actions. Consider this, as you hear the following true story.

Reading

Jean Thompson stood in front of her class of ten-year-olds on the very first day of school in September and told the children a lie. Like most teachers, she looked at her pupils and said that she loved each of them the same, that she would treat them all alike. This was impossible because there, in front of her, slumped in his seat on the third row, was a little boy named Teddy Stoddard.

Mrs Thompson had watched Teddy the year before and noticed he didn't play well with the other children, that his clothes were unkempt and that he constantly needed a bath. And Teddy was unpleasant. It got to the point during the first few months that she would actually take delight in marking his papers with a broad red pen, making bold X's and then highlighting the 'F' at the top of the paper. Because Teddy was a sullen little boy, no one else seemed to like him either.

At the school where Mrs Thompson taught, she was required to read each child's personal records. She left Teddy's until last. When she opened his file, she found a surprise. His first-year teacher had written, 'Teddy is a bright, inquisitive child with a ready laugh. He does his work neatly and has good manners. He is a joy to be around.' His second-year teacher had written, 'Teddy is an excellent student, well-liked by all his classmates, but he is troubled because his mother has a terminal illness and

60

life at home must be a struggle.' His third-year teacher had noted, 'Teddy continues to work hard but his mother's death has been hard on him. He tries to do his best but his father doesn't show much interest and his home life will soon affect him if some steps aren't taken.' Teddy's fourth-year teacher had commented, 'Teddy is withdrawn and doesn't show much interest in school. He doesn't have many friends and often falls asleep in class. He is tardy and could become a more serious problem.'

By now Mrs Thompson realized the extent of the problem, but Christmas was approaching fast. On the day before the holidays began she was suddenly forced to focus again on Teddy Stoddard. Her children brought her presents, all in beautiful ribbon and bright paper, except Teddy's, which was clumsily wrapped in the heavy, brown paper of a grocery bag. Mrs Thompson took pains to open it in the middle of the other presents. Some of the children started to laugh when she found a cheap bracelet with some of the stones missing, and a bottle that was one-quarter full of cologne. She stifled the children's laughter while she exclaimed how pretty the bracelet was, putting it on, and dabbing some of the perfume on her wrist.

Teddy Stoddard stayed behind after class just long enough to say, 'Mrs Thompson, today you smelled just like my mum used to.'

After the children left, she cried for at least an hour. On that very day, she stopped teaching reading, writing and speaking. Instead, she began to teach children. Jean Thompson paid particular attention to Teddy. As she worked with him his mind seemed to come alive. The more she encouraged him the faster he responded. On those days when there was an important test, Mrs Thompson would remember that perfume. By the end of the year he had become one of the highest-achieving children in the class and, well, he had also somewhat become the 'pet' of that teacher who had once vowed to love all of her children exactly the same.

Personal values

A year later she found a note under her door, from Teddy, telling her that of all the teachers he'd had in primary school, she was his favourite. Six years went by before she got another note from Teddy. He then wrote that he had finished secondary school, third in his class, and she was still his favourite teacher of all time. Three years after that, she got another letter, saying that while things had been tough at times, he'd stayed in college, had stuck with it, and would graduate from university with the highest of honours. He assured Mrs Thompson she was still his favourite teacher.

Four more years passed and yet another letter came. This time he explained that after he got his bachelor's degree, he decided to go a little further. The letter explained that she was still his favourite teacher but that now his name was a little longer. The letter was signed, Theodore F. Stoddard, MD.

The story doesn't end there. You see, there was yet another letter that spring. Teddy said he'd met this girl and was to be married. He explained that his father had died a couple of years ago and he was wondering if Mrs Thompson might agree to sit in the pew usually reserved for the mother of the groom. And on that day, she wore that bracelet, the one with several stones missing. And on that special day, Jean Thompson smelled just like Teddy remembered his mother smelling.

Reflections

- To exercise compassion is to put yourself in someone else's shoes; to experience life as they see it.

- *Charity is incumbent on each person every day. Charity is assisting anyone, moving and carrying their wares, saying a good word.*

    (Muhammad, 570–632, Prophet of Islam)

- Choose to watch out for those in need. Choose to show kindness today.

22. The power of love to change lives

Theme: Love

Introduction

Benjamin Franklin (1706–1790), an American statesman at the time of the War of Independence, once said, 'If you would be loved, love and be loveable.'

Reading

Once upon a time there lived a young orphan girl. Her parents had died when she was a baby and she was left in the world alone, with no one to love or to be loved by. One day, feeling lonely and sad, she walked through the wood near her town. She saw, caught in a thorn bush, a butterfly anxiously fluttering, trying to get free. However, the more the butterfly tried to become free the more it hurt itself, tearing its wings on the thorns. Carefully the young orphan girl separated the thorns from the butterfly, freeing it from its agony. Once free, instead of flying away the butterfly turned into a beautiful fairy.

The young girl could hardly believe what she was seeing. 'For your kindness,' the fairy said to the girl, 'I will grant you one wish.' The little girl thought for a moment and then replied, 'I wish to be happy.' The fairy granted her wish and flew away never to be seen again.

A sudden change came over the girl. All of a sudden she felt a warm glow inside. She no longer felt lonely and scared. Instead, she felt love for all. As she grew up everyone wanted to know the secret of her happiness. However, she only smiled and replied, 'The secret is that when I was a young girl I listened to a good fairy.' She would say no more.

Personal values

Years later, when the girl was old and on her deathbed, her friends begged her to tell them her secret. How was she so happy all of the time? The lovely old lady simply smiled and said, 'The fairy told me that everyone, be they rich or poor, old or young, has need of me. However secure or insecure people are, they all need me to love them. That is my secret.'

Reflections

- *We can only learn to love by loving.*
  (*The Bell*, Iris Murdoch)

- *If I can stop one heart from breaking I shall not live in vain.*
  (Emily Dickenson, 1830–1886, American poet)

- *Truly loving another means letting go of all expectations. It means full acceptance, even celebration of another's personhood.*
  (Karen Casey)

23. The love programme

Theme: The nature of love

Introduction

The following reading is a fictional conversation between a computer company, called Heart Systems Software, and one of its customers. It explores the nature of love and the effects which love can have in a person's life.

Reading

Customer Service: Hello, you have reached the Heart Systems Software Company help desk. How may I help you?

Customer: I just received your latest program, LOVE version 4.0 ... you know ... the freebee. I don't understand it. First, can you tell me what the program does, and then explain how to install it?

Customer Service: LOVE is a unique program. It attaches to your operating system and runs silently in the background, you will never see LOVE on your monitor or your toolbar, but you will notice its affect on every application you may have. It makes the good programs run more smoothly and greatly restricts and/or deletes the bad ones.

Customer: Wow! That sounds great. How does LOVE make my machine run more smoothly?

Personal values

Customer Service: Well, good files, like COMPLIMENT, ENCOURAGEMENT, and KINDWORD will play frequently. Also, FORGIVENESS.EXE will come into action every time there is an external violation.

Customer: But what about the bad programs?

Customer Service: Good question. LOVE searches your memory for programs like HATE.DOC, BITTERNESS.EXE, SELFISH.DOC and SPITE.EXE. These programs can't be entirely deleted from your hard drive, but LOVE overpowers them. LOVE stops their commands from being executed and runs its own instructions. You will no longer hear INSULT.EXE and you won't be able to write with the fonts BADWORDS12 or HARSHNESS10.

Customer: I think I'm ready to install now. What do I do first?

Customer Service: The first step is to open your external Hard-drive Email And Remote Terminal (HEART). Have you located your HEART?

Customer: Yes I have, but there are several programs running right now. Is it okay to install while they are running?

Customer Service: What programs are running?

Customer: Let me see ... I have PASTHURT.EXE, LOWESTEEM.EXE, GRUDGE.EXE and RESENTMENT.DOC running right now.

Customer Service: No problem. LOVE will automatically erase PASTHURT.EXE from your current operating system. It may remain in your permanent memory, but it will no longer disrupt other programs. LOVE will eventually overwrite LOWESTEEM.EXE with a module of its own called HIGHESTEEM.EXE. However, you have to turn off GRUDGE.EXE and RESENTMENT.DOC completely. Those programs prevent LOVE from being properly installed. Can you turn those off madam?

Customer: I don't know how to turn them off. Can you tell me how?

Customer Service: My pleasure. Go to your Start menu and invoke FORGIVENESS.EXE. Do this as many times as necessary until GRUDGE.EXE and RESENTMENT.DOC have been completely erased.

Customer: Okay, I've done that. LOVE has started installing itself automatically. Is that normal?

Customer Service: Yes it is. You should receive a message that says it will reinstall for the life of your HEART. Do you see that message?

Customer: Yes I do. Hey! My HEART is filling up with really cool files. SMILE.MPG is playing on my monitor right now and it shows that WARMTH.DOC, PEACE.EXE and CONTENTMENT.DOC are copying themselves all over my HEART!

Customer Service: Then LOVE is installed and running. You should be able to handle it from here. One more thing before I go.

Personal values

Customer: Yes?

Customer Service: LOVE is freeware. Be sure to give it and its various modules to everybody you meet. They will in turn share it with other people.

Customer: I will. Thank you for your help.

Reflections

- What do you learn about the nature of love from this reading?

- What obstacles stand in the way of love? How would you go about removing these obstacles in your life?

- *One of the teachers of the law came to Jesus and asked, 'Of all the commandments, which is the most important?' 'The most important one,' answered Jesus, 'is this … "Love the Lord your God with all your heart" … The second is this, "Love your neighbour as yourself."'*

(Mark 12:28–31)

24. Two babes in a manger

Theme: The meaning of Christmas

Introduction

In 1994 the Russian Department of Education invited two Christians to come and teach about their faith in schools, prisons and a large orphanage. At the orphanage about 100 boys and girls had been left, abandoned and abused by their parents. The two Christians relate the following story in their own words.

Reading

In was nearing the holiday season, and time for the orphans to hear, for the first time, the traditional story of Christmas. We told them about Mary and Joseph arriving in Bethlehem. Finding no room in the inn, the couple went to a stable where the baby Jesus was born and placed in a manger. Throughout the story the children and orphanage staff sat in amazement as they listened. Some sat on the edges of their stools, trying to grasp every word. Completing the story, we gave the children three small pieces of cardboard to make a crude manger. Each child was given a small paper square. Following instructions, the children tore the paper and carefully laid strips in the manger for straw. Small squares of flannel, cut from a worn-out nightgown a woman was throwing away, were used for the baby's blanket. A doll-like baby was cut from felt. The orphans were busy assembling their manger as I walked among them to see if they needed any help.

All went well until I got to one table where little Misha sat. He looked about six years old and had finished his project. As I looked at the little boy's manger I was startled to see not one but two babes in the manger. I asked why there were two. Crossing his arms in front of him, and looking at this completed manger scene, Misha began to repeat the story very seriously. For such a young boy, who had only heard the Christmas story once, he

Personal values

related the happenings accurately until he came to the part where Mary put the baby Jesus in the manger.

Then Misha started to ad lib. He made up his own ending to the story as he said, 'And when Maria laid the baby in the manger Jesus looked at me and asked me if I had a place to stay. I told him I have no mamma and I have no papa, so I didn't have any place to stay. Then Jesus told me I could stay with him. But I told him I couldn't, because I didn't have a gift to give him like everybody else did. But I wanted to stay with Jesus so much, so I thought about what I had that maybe I could use for a gift. I thought maybe that if I kept him warm, that would be a good gift. So I asked Jesus, "If I keep you warm, will that be a good enough gift?" And Jesus told me, "If you keep me warm that will be the best gift anybody ever gave me." So I got into the manger, and then Jesus looked at me and he told me I could stay with him – for always.'

As little Misha finished his story, his eyes brimmed full of tears that splashed down his little cheeks. Putting his hand over his face, his head dropped to the table and his shoulders shook as he sobbed and sobbed. The little orphan had found someone who would never abandon nor abuse him, someone who would stay with him *for always*. I've learned that it's not what you have in your life but who you have in your life that counts.

Reflection

- How true is that last sentiment, 'It's not what you have in your life but who you have in your life that counts'?

25. A lot of hot air

Theme: Having manners

Introduction

When we say that someone has good manners we are praising them for their politeness and social concern for others. Good manners can show itself in many ways, for example:

- *opening the door for someone to go through*
- *not pushing into queues*
- *saying 'please' and 'thank you'.*

Good manners are not just about being polite. They help the wheel of life to turn more easily.

Reading

The Master was certainly not a stickler for etiquette and good manners but there was always a natural courtesy and grace in his dealings with others.

A young disciple was once very rude to a traffic policeman as he drove the Master home one night. In self-defence he said, 'I'd rather be myself and let people know exactly how I feel. Politeness is nothing but a lot of hot air.'

'True enough,' said the Master pleasantly, 'but that's what we have in our automobile tyres and see how it eases the bumps.'

(*One Minute Nonsense*, Anthony de Mello)

Personal values

Reflections

- *A man's behaviour is the index of the man, and his discourse is the index of his understanding.*

  (Ali, c.600–661, first Imam of the Sh'iah branch of Islam, the fourth caliph)

- Make a list of 'good manners'. Try practising one of them today and notice how it changes people's reactions to you.

26. Sparky

Theme: Perseverance

Introduction

How do you react when you find things difficult? Do you keep on trying, or do you give up easily?

Perseverance is the commitment to carry on at something even when it is difficult or tiresome. The following true story illustrates this quality.

Reading

Sparky was born in Minneapolis, Minnesota, USA. At school he was a poor student. When he was thirteen years old he failed every subject. He managed to achieve nought per cent in his physics examination. He didn't do much better in his non-academic subjects. However, he did manage to make the school's golf team, but then went on to lose the only important match of the season.

During his teenage years Sparky found it difficult to mix with others. He didn't really have any good friends. In fact, he was a bit of a loner and was always amazed when anyone said hello to him. In many people's eyes Sparky was a loser. He had even come to terms with the fact that he would not really get anywhere in life. He almost expected to fail every time he started something new.

However, one thing did matter to Sparky, and that was his drawing. He used to spend hours drawing cartoons, even though no one else appreciated his skills. Even when he submitted cartoons for the school paper they were turned down. This did not put him off. He was determined to be a professional cartoonist.

Personal values

After finishing High School he completed a correspondence course. He sent samples of his artwork to the Walt Disney Studios, only to be rejected by them too. However, he did not give up. He decided to write his autobiography in cartoons. He described his life – the story of a little boy who was always a loser. The cartoon character would soon become famous worldwide. Today *Peanuts* is one of the most popular comic strips in history, appearing in more than 2000 newspapers and translated into more than twenty languages.

Sparky, the boy who was such a loser at school, was actually Charles M. Schultz. His cartoon character was Charlie Brown. Schultz went on to receive many awards for his cartoon characters.

Reflections

- If at first you don't succeed, try, try and try again.

- At some time or other many of us can identify with Sparky – his feelings of being lost and alone. We all feel at times as though it is no good trying, we might as well give up. However, like Sparky, we need to believe in our own ability and to persevere at the skill we have been given. It might be the skill of getting on well with people, of being a good listener; it might be an artistic or musical skill.

- *If there is no dull and determined effort, there will be no brilliant achievement.*
  (Hsun-tzu, 298–238 BCE, Chinese philosopher)

- *No individual or people can achieve anything without industry, suffering and sacrifice.*
  (Fatima Jinna, 1893–1967, Pakistani politician)

- *Before proceeding, one must reach.*
  (West African proverb)

27. Michelangelo and the Duccio block

Theme: Overcoming obstacles

Introduction

One of the things that distinguish humans from animals is that they have the ability to be creative. All of us make creative decisions on a daily basis.

This story illustrates how we can each use our creativity to overcome obstacles in life.

Reading

Duccio was one of the greatest sculptors in Italy in the fifteenth century. He worked in the beautiful city of Florence. In 1450 a huge piece of marble was quarried out of the mountains near Carrara and taken to his workshop. The city council had commissioned Duccio to sculpt the magnificent figure of Hercules.

Duccio set to work on this masterpiece, but at one point became distracted and made a wrong cut in the marble. He damaged the piece of marble at its core. Looking at the vast block of white marble Duccio could not think of any way he could salvage the figure of Hercules. He covered it over with cloths and left the piece outside the cathedral. It became known as the Duccio block.

Over the next fifty years many sculptors came to visit the Duccio block. They each measured it and contemplated how they could cut a figure out of it without having to use the central damaged part. All went away downhearted. The marble was too deeply damaged for them to rescue it.

Personal values

However, in 1501 the great Michelangelo visited Florence and studied the block. As he examined the piece he was inspired: if he tipped the block forward at an angle of 20 degrees and cut a figure with hips swivelled away from the damaged area, a human body could be carved. And then he had another inspiration – he knew exactly what figure it would be: David in the act of throwing the stone at Goliath. The hips would be swivelled away from the centre as David turned to throw the stone at the giant. Suddenly the obstacles in the block were its strengths.

It took Michelangelo over two years to complete his sculpture. The piece is colossal. The Old Testament hero is shown as an energetic, naked youth, very muscular and alert. David looks into the distance as though he is weighing up his opponent, Goliath. Today it is recognized as one of the greatest pieces of art.

Reflections

- Obstacles do not need to be barriers in life. They can be opportunities to be truly creative, to stretch oneself into new things.

- *God has given each normal person a capacity to achieve some end. True, some are endowed with more talent than others, but God has left none of us talentless.*
  (Martin Luther King Jr, 1929–1968, American civil rights leader)

28. The little old lady

Theme: Respect for each other

Introduction

Each person deserves our respect, for each person is unique and of infinite value. However, sometimes we judge people by the way they look, without trying to see them for who they really are on the inside. This can lead to great misunderstanding, as this story illustrates.

Reading

One day a mother took all of her young children to the beach. It was a beautifully sunny day. As the children were playing in the sand, making their own fortress and castle, an old lady appeared in the distance. As she came closer the mother noticed that she was dressed in rags. She looked as though she had not washed for days. She was muttering to herself as she bent low to pick up things from the beach. She had a bag over her shoulder that already looked full.

The mother called to her children not to go near the old lady. As she passed by she greeted each of the children and gave them a lovely smile. But the children did not respond: they just carried on making their castle in the sand. The old lady moved past continuing to pick up things from the beach.

A week later they read about the old lady in the local newspaper. She had died from a heart attack. As the mother read the story she learnt that the old lady had made it her life-long task to comb the beach for pieces of glass and tin. For the last fifty years she had spent every day cleaning the beach so that children would not cut their feet.

Personal values

Reflection

- Appearances can be deceptive. Learn to look into people's hearts, to see their goodness and beauty.

29. You can do it!

Theme: Self-confidence – making life count

Introduction

What's it like being a teenager? Do you have confidence in yourself or do you write yourself off? One fifteen-year-old girl described herself as 'a semi-relevant teenager not even above the age of consent'. But it doesn't have to be this way.

Sometimes when you are going through school it is easy to feel as though you don't count, that no one listens to you. The following reading is about a thirteen-year-old girl who made life count.

Reading

Her real name was Annelies Marie, although most people called her Anne – well at least when they weren't annoyed with her. There was nothing extraordinary about Anne – she was not stunningly beautiful nor was she the most brilliant student. Like most other teenagers, Anne grabbed hold of life: one day she would be as high as a kite, the next in a dark mood. Like most thirteen-year-old girls she wondered what it would be like to be in love, and when she had her first kiss she wrote a whole page in her diary describing it.

It was this diary which was to make her famous. She has gone down in history as the girl who wrote a diary of what it was like hiding in an attic. You may know her as Anne Frank. She spent two years in that attic, situated above her father's grocery business.

It was a summer afternoon in 1942 when she and her family gathered up a few belongings and entered the attic. It was 1 August 1944 when the Nazi police burst the door down, then

Personal values

shoved Anne and her family down the steps and into the waiting cars. No one immediately noticed the red-checked diary left behind. '(No one) will be interested in the unbosoming of a thirteen-year-old schoolgirl,' she wrote in the first pages of her diary. She was wrong. When she was sixteen she was struck by typhus and died in Bergen-Belsen concentration camp. Years later over 2000 young people would visit the mass grave in which she was buried to lay flowers on it, and her diary has become an international bestseller and movie. That diary has been translated into more than thirty languages. The attic in Amsterdam is now a museum visited by thousands each year.

The diary was found a week after Anne's arrest, by a family friend who gave it to Anne's father after the war. He was the only member of her family to be found alive by the liberators at the end of the war. In Anne's diary you can see the encroaching darkness of the war through the eyes of a bright-eyed thirteen-year-old girl. Even as the darkness enfolds her, Anne writes happy stories about playing ping-pong and feeling the sun on her face. She says she knows that people are basically kind and, no matter what happens, good will triumph.

Reflections

- As we grow up it is easy to lose our sense of fun and enjoyment about life. Like Anne, celebrate the good things in life today. Have confidence in yourself. Speak out for goodness and kindness. Make a difference.

- Why not start keeping a diary where you can record your thoughts and ideas?

- Make life count – only you can do it!

30. Aristotle's challenge

Theme: Schooling the emotions – self-control

Introduction

As an introductory activity, role-play with a pupil a scene in which the teacher is getting angry with a student. The teacher is losing control. The student responds aggressively.

Ask, 'What is going on in the scene that you have just witnessed? What emotions did the participants show? Did they handle themselves well? How could they have handled themselves better?'

We all find ourselves in situations in which we react in ways that we know are not helpful. But how do we change our reactions?

The Greek philosopher Aristotle (384–322 BCE) argued that we all should learn to handle our emotions well. In The Nicomachean Ethics *he wrote, 'Anyone can become angry – that is easy. But to be angry with the right person, to the right degree, at the right time, for the right purpose, and in the right way – this is not easy.' What Aristotle says about anger applies to any emotion. His challenge was to learn to manage emotions with intelligence.*

As you listen to the following stories compare how people handled their emotions in them.

Reading 1

The first reading comes from Buddhism. The Buddha taught his followers to cultivate an attitude of loving-kindness (metta) towards each other and all living creatures.

One day a rude and angry young man came up to the Buddha and started insulting him. The Buddha did not get upset. Instead, he asked the young man, 'If you buy a gift for someone, and that person does not take it, to whom does the gift belong?' The

Personal values

young man replied gruffly, 'It would belong to me because I bought the gift.' The Buddha, with a smile all over his face, replied, 'That is right. And it is exactly the same with your anger. If you become angry with me but I do not become affronted, then the anger falls back on you. Then you are the one who becomes unhappy, not me. If you want to stop hurting yourself you must get rid of your anger and become loving instead. When you hate others you yourself become unhappy.'

Reading 2

In stark contrast to the first reading, listen to these extracts from a recent newspaper.

- *At a local school two sixteen-year-olds went on the rampage, vandalizing teachers' cars and smashing classroom windows. The reason? They felt they were misfits in the school, rejected by both teachers and fellow students, and wanted to be heard.*

- *A report shows that 57 per cent of the murderers of children under twelve are their own parents or step-parents. In almost half these cases the parents defended themselves by saying that they were merely trying to discipline their child.*

- *Road rage claims another victim. A man in his thirties was killed last night when another driver rammed his car off the road. The driver of the car defended himself by saying that the victim had cut in front of him, trying to overtake on a narrow lane.*

Each day newspapers present stories of people whose emotions are out of control.

Reflections

- What does it mean to become angry with the right person, to the right degree, at the right time, for the right purpose and in the right way? Is it possible?

- Next time you become angry try the following six steps for impulse control.

  1. Stop.

  2. Calm down and give yourself time to think before you act.

  3. Get in touch with how you feel – if necessary, put it into words.

  4. Think of lots of solutions.

  5. Think ahead to the consequences.

  6. Try the best plan.

- *If you yield to your anger, you only cease to be civil.*
  (Abu'l-Fath al-Busti, d.1009, Persian poet)

31. The bramble bush

Theme: The struggle between good and evil

Introduction

As we grow up, it becomes more difficult to uproot bad habits. Just think about people who eat too much and want to lose weight. The longer they leave it the more difficult it becomes to stick to a diet.

The religions of the world teach that the struggle with evil is ongoing. We have to fight those things that are not healthy, day in and day out. This Muslim parable reminds us that the longer we wait to fight a wrong habit the harder it is to defeat it.

Reading

A man once planted a bramble bush right in the middle of the road. Although people told him to tear it up, he refused. As a result, people who went past it tore their clothes and wounded their feet on the brambles that were shed from it.

Even the mayor of the town told the man to dig up the bramble bush. 'One day, I will,' replied the man, but in the meantime the bush grew bigger and bigger, doing more and more harm.

The mayor accused the man of breaking his promise. The man turned round to the bush and said that he wished he could dig it up, but it had now grown far too big and he hadn't the necessary strength. The mayor replied, 'The longer you leave it the more powerful that evil bush will become and the weaker you will become. Be quick, therefore, and do not waste your time.'

As the man started to dig he realized that he had left the job too late. The roots were too deep.

Reflections

- The bush is like any of our bad habits. The more we leave them alone and do not dig them up, the more firmly they take their hold on our lives. They become so powerful that they become more and more difficult to uproot. Be warned!

- *According as a man acts and walks in the path of life, so he becomes. He that does good becomes good; he that does evil becomes evil. By pure actions he becomes pure; by evil actions he becomes evil.*
  (Brihadaranyaka Upanishad, c.600–300 BCE, sacred philosophical Hindu literature)

- *He who is able to conquer others is powerful; he who is able to conquer himself is more powerful.*
  (Lao-tzu, c.604–531 BCE, Chinese philosopher and founder of Taoism, 'Tao-te ching')

32. The marshmallow test

Theme: Self-restraint – motivating oneself and controlling impulses

Introduction

We all know what it feels like to lack all motivation to do something. Just think of the last time you put off doing homework. How easy was it to sit down and get on with it? How tempted were you to be distracted by television or what was happening outside?

We only have to look at the great achievers in life to see how important it is to motivate ourselves to do something – even when we don't feel like it. Look at the great athletes and musicians around today. Throughout their lives they have devoted themselves to strenuous training routines in order to reach the top. This reading records an experiment which illustrated the importance of self-motivation and control.

Reading

In the 1960s psychologist Walter Mischel carried out an experiment to test how important self-motivation and control were. It became known as the marshmallow test.

A group of four-year-olds were offered a challenge. The children were told that the experimenter had to go on an errand. If they were willing to wait until he returned they would be rewarded with two marshmallows. However, if they couldn't wait they would be given one marshmallow straight away but would not receive another one on his return. Some of the four-year-olds showed great self-restraint. They were motivated by the possible reward of two marshmallows. They did everything to stop themselves touching the one marshmallow in front of them. The experimenter was away for twenty minutes, and that must have seemed a very long time to the children. They talked with each other, shut their eyes so as not to be tempted – anything as long as they didn't miss out on the reward. However, some of them couldn't help themselves: they ate their one marshmallow within seconds of the experimenter leaving the room.

These four-year-olds were tracked down ten years later. The psychologist observed that those who had previously showed self-control in resisting the marshmallows were now, as teenagers, more emotionally and socially competent. They dealt better with frustrations in life and rarely gave up when faced with challenges. They were more confident and took the initiative. Ten years later they were still able to postpone instant gratification in order to pursue their goals. The third or so who grabbed hold of the marshmallows when they were four had fewer of these qualities. They were more easily upset by frustrations and very prone to acting out their impulses, with much less self-restraint. Furthermore, they were still unable to postpone gratification.

What is more surprising is the progress of these same four-year-olds when they were checked again at eighteen, when they had finished their schooling. Those who had waited patiently at four years of age were the most successful students. They were more able to put their ideas into words, make plans and follow them through.

Reflections

- Suggest ways in which the skill to motivate yourself is important in life.

- Discuss why it is important to learn how to control your impulses.

Personal values

- *The trouble with being number one in the world – at anything – is that it takes a certain mentality to attain that position in the first place, and that is something of a driving, perfectionist attitude, so that once you do achieve number one, you don't relax and enjoy it.*

  (Billie Jean King, b.1943, American athlete)

- *Go for the moon. If you don't get it, you'll still be heading for a star.*

  (Willis Reed, b.1942, American athlete)

33. The king and his hawk

Theme: Self-control

Introduction

Have you ever heard the saying 'Think before you act'? This story, from the time of the Mongol empire, illustrates how important it is to do so.

Reading

Genghis Khan (1162–1227 – his name means 'ruler of all'), founder of the Mongol empire, was a great king who led his army into China and Persia. One day the king and his friends went into the woods on a hunting trip. In those days hawks were trained to hunt. At a command from their masters they would fly up into the air and search for their prey. They would swoop down on any rabbits and wild animals they saw.

That particular day, the hawks found less prey than expected. In early afternoon, as the sun was starting to descend in the sky, the hunters began to make their way back home. The king chose a different route from his party, wishing to spend some time alone. It had been a hot day and he soon became thirsty. His pet hawk had flown off, making its own way home. As the king journeyed on he came across some water trickling down a rock. He climbed down from his horse and took a metal cup out of his saddle bag. He held it to catch each drop of the refreshing water. It took a long time for the cup to fill to the brim. Just as he was about to put the cup to his lips he heard a swishing sound in the air. Suddenly, his favourite hawk swooped down, knocking the cup out of the king's hand.

The king started again, holding the cup to catch the slow-running drops. When the cup was nearly full he held it towards

Personal values

his lips. Again his hawk appeared, as if from nowhere, knocking his arm and causing him to drop the water. At this the king began to grow angry. For a third time he collected water from the rock – this time he was so thirsty that he only collected half a cup. But again, just as he was about to drink the water, his hawk caused the cup to fall to the ground. The king became furious and took out his sword. With one swift blow he struck his hawk, piercing its flesh. The next moment the poor hawk lay dying on the ground.

'Now at least I can drink the water.' However, the cup had fallen between two rocks. The king climbed slowly to the top of the cliff and at last reached the source of the water. There was a pool of water but lying in the centre of the pool were the remains of a dead snake, one of the most poisonous. The king stopped in his tracks. He forgot his thirst. He thought only of the poor, dead hawk that had saved his life. 'He was my best friend, and I have killed him.' He climbed down the rocks, gently picked up his pet hawk and put it in his saddle bag. He slowly made his way back to his palace. 'I have learned an important lesson today, and that is never to do anything in anger.'

Reflections

- When we are under the influence of a strong emotion, such as anger, it is easy to do things which we later regret. It is important to be in control of our emotions and not let our emotions control us.

- *The conquest of oneself is better than the conquest of all others.*

    (Dhammapada, third century BCE,
    collection of ancient Buddhist teachings)

34. Controlling your temper

Theme: Self-control

Introduction

Do you lose your temper? What causes you to 'fly off the handle'? This true story is about controlling a temper.

Reading

There was a little boy with a bad temper. His father gave him a bag of nails and told him that he should hammer a nail in the back fence every time he lost his temper. After the first day the boy had driven 37 nails into the fence. Then the number gradually dwindled down.

He discovered it was easier to hold his temper than to drive those nails into the fence.

Finally the day came when the boy didn't lose his temper at all.

He told his father, who immediately suggested that the boy should pull out one nail for each day that he was able to hold his temper. The days passed and the young boy was finally able to tell his father that all the nails were gone.

The father took his son by the hand and led him to the fence. He said, 'You have done well, my son, but look at the holes in the fence. The fence will never be the same. When you say things in anger, they leave scars just like these. You can put a knife in a man and draw it out. It won't matter how many times you say you are sorry, the wound will still be there. A verbal wound is as bad as a physical one.'

Personal values

Reflections

- *One must fight for a life of action, not reaction.*

  (Rita Mae Brown)

- *If your mind is dominated by anger, you will lose the best part of the human brain: wisdom, the ability to decide between what is right and what is wrong. Anger is the most serious problem facing the world today.*

  (*Ocean of Wisdom: Guidelines for Living*, Dalai Lama)

35. The greedy monk

Theme: Motives are important when we are trying to understand someone's actions

Introduction

When you do something good do you want others to notice? Sometimes the greatest good is done in secret.

People are sometimes misunderstood when they try to do good. This story illustrates the importance of not judging a person's motives and character until you know their true qualities.

Reading

Gessen was a Buddhist monk. He was also an exceptionally talented artist. Before he started work on any painting, however, he always demanded payment in advance. And his fees were exorbitant, so he became known as the 'greedy monk'.

A lady once sent for him to have a painting done. Gessen said, 'How much will you pay me?' The lady happened to be entertaining a patron at the time. She said, 'Any sum you ask for. But the painting must be done right here and now, before me.'

Gessen set to work at once and when the painting was completed he asked for the highest sum he had ever charged. As the lady was giving him his money, she said to her patron, 'This man is supposed to be a monk, but all he thinks of is money. His talent is exceptional, but he has a filthy, money-loving mind. How does one exhibit the canvas of a filthy, money-loving man like that? His work is only good enough for my underclothing!'

With that she flung a petticoat at him and asked him to paint a picture on it. Gessen asked the usual question before he started the work. 'How much will you give me?' 'Oh, any sum you ask

Personal values

for,' said the lady. Gessen named his price, painted the picture, shamelessly pocketed the money and walked away.

Many years later, quite by chance, someone found out why Gessen was so greedy for money. Devastating famine often struck his home province. The rich would do nothing to help the poor, so Gessen had secretly built barns in the area and had them filled with grain for such emergencies. No one knew where the grain came from or who the benefactor of the province was.

Gessen also wanted money to repair the road leading to his village from the city, many miles away. It was in such bad condition that ox carts could not move on it; this caused much suffering to the aged and the infirm when they needed to get to the city. Gessen had the road repaired.

His final project was a temple for meditation that Gessen's teacher had always wanted to build but could not afford. Gessen built the temple as a token of gratitude to his revered teacher.

After the 'greedy monk' had built the barns, the road and the temple, he threw away his paint and brushes, retired to the mountains to give himself to the contemplative life, and never painted another canvas again.

(*Taking Flight*, Anthony de Mello)

Reflections

- There is an old saying, 'You can't judge a book by its cover'.

- *Actions will be judged according to their intentions.*
  (Muhammad, 570–632, Prophet of Islam)

36. Beauty within

Theme: Self-esteem – learning to like oneself

Introduction

Ask pupils to put their hands up if they feel good about themselves today. Ask how many of them find this an easy question. How many like themselves?

Today's reading shows how important it is to believe in oneself.

Reading

The great Italian artist, Michelangelo, was asked by an admirer, 'How do you create such beautiful sculptures?' Michelangelo replied, 'The beauty is already there, my friend. I do not create beauty, God creates beauty. I merely chip away the surrounding marble so as to reveal the beauty. The beauty is already within. It is already perfectly in place.'

The same is true about each one of us. Deep inside each one of us there is beauty, something of unique worth. And yet each of us hides this inner beauty under layers of dirt. We fall into bad and negative habits. We all do things we wish we didn't. It is easy to lose sight of the beauty in our heart. Sometimes people lose complete sight of their own beauty and start to think they are worthless. At other times, people allow others to tell them that they are no good.

Personal values

Reflections

- Today make an especial effort to see the beauty in yourself and in each person you meet.

- *No one can make you feel inferior without your consent.*
  (Eleanor Roosevelt, 1884–1962, American humanitarian and wife of the US President)

- *Beware of allowing a tactless word, a rebuttal, a rejection to obliterate the whole sky.*
  (Anais Nin, 1903–1977, American writer)

37. IQ or EI?

Theme: The importance of emotional intelligence

Introduction

What should schools be teaching you in order for you to be successful in life? Are there things that you need to learn to survive in life which school does not presently teach you?

This reading explores the importance of those things which are above and beyond IQ and asks the question – what are schools doing to prepare you for life?

Reading

Many people believe that a person's IQ (intelligence quotient) determines their success. However, research suggests that IQ contributes only about 20 per cent to the factors that determine success in life. Consider the many people who leave school with few academic qualifications but go on to lead successful businesses and parent flourishing families.

There are many characteristics in life other than IQ which predict success. Some very important ones include the ability to:

- handle one's own feelings well and deal effectively with other people's feelings

- motivate oneself and to persist at a task despite frustrations

- control impulse and to regulate one's moods

- understand other people and build strong and lasting relationships.

Personal values

Very few of these characteristics are tested in the school curriculum, but it is often these abilities which determine success.

Without these personal qualities it is likely that you will make poor choices about who to marry, what job to take and how to handle stress. In a real sense all of us have two minds: a rational mind that thinks and an emotional mind that feels. Tests of IQ concentrate on the rational – language and mathematical skills. Emotional intelligence, on the other hand, includes a range of personal qualities:

- *self-awareness* – understanding your own feelings as they are happening, for example, being able to recognize that you are becoming angry or jealous before actually acting on those feelings

- *ability to handle your emotions well* – having self-control

- *self-motivation* – forcing yourself to do something even when you don't want to

- *recognizing emotions in others* – a key 'people skill', the ability to feel others' needs, to read their faces and recognize their emotions

- *ability to handle relationships well* – to get the best out of people you are living and working with.

Reflections

- Have you ever been told, 'Think before you act'? What does it mean? Are your actions prompted more often by your emotions (doing what you feel) or by your head (thinking about issues first)?

- *It is with the heart that one sees rightly; what is essential is invisible to the eye.*
  (*The Little Prince*, Antoine De Saint Exupery)

Do you agree?

38. Are you passion's slave?

Theme: Understanding our own emotions

Introduction

Do you ever feel out of control, as though your emotions are taking over? Do you act on impulse, and if so what makes you do so? Are you ever tempted to justify yourself by saying 'I can't help myself'?

Television and newspapers often display the results of emotions out of control, of people who act out of impulse without thinking first. The following reading talks about the importance of understanding and being in control of the emotions.

Reading

The ability to master your emotions and passions and not be their slave has been recognized as a virtue since early times. The Romans and early Christians referred to this virtue as 'temperance'. It referred to the ability to show emotional balance. It is not a matter of living without passions, trying to press down all the big emotions. In fact, many emotions are valuable. What is required is a way of dealing with emotions skillfully, being in control of the emotions rather than letting *them* be in control.

In Shakespeare's play *Hamlet*, the king praises this ability to control emotions which he sees in his friend Horatio.

Thou hast been …
A man that Fortune's buffets and rewards
Has taken with equal thanks … Give me that man
That is not Passion's slave, and I will wear him
In my heart's core, aye, in my heart of hearts
As I do thee…

Managing your emotions is something of a full-time job. The first step is to understand your emotions and passions and their effect within you. One way of doing this is to spend some time listening to your emotions. Instead of acting on impulse, observe how emotions are making you feel. Become a watcher of your own emotions. At times, be like a lawyer and cross-examine your emotions: 'Why am I feeling like this?'

People can't often choose or control when they are going to be swept away by an emotion. What they can control is how they manage the emotion and how long it lasts. Research suggests that the emotion that people are worst at controlling is anger. Anger is very seductive because it energizes us.

We have to decide whether we are going to be controlled by the emotions or whether we are going to manage them skilfully.

Reflection

- Our emotions are experiences that happen to us. They are not who we are. Buddhists say, 'I am with anger,' as opposed to 'I am angry,' and 'I am with sadness,' not 'I am sad.' They say, 'I am with jealousy,' as opposed to 'I am jealous.' Naming the emotion you are living with helps you to create a distance between who you are and the emotion you are experiencing. Such a tactic helps you to work with your emotions and not let the emotions take you over. Try it!

39. Monks in the heat of battle

Theme: Taking responsibility for our moods

Introduction

We catch feelings from one another. Have you noticed how a person's bad mood can affect all the other people in their company? On the other hand, notice how people who are calm and peaceful are good to be around. We use words such as 'popular' and 'good fun' for people who we like to be with, because they make us feel good. This reading illustrates how feelings can be contagious and turn the course of events.

Reading

This event took place early in the Vietnam War (1959–1975). A group of American soldiers were rooted in the middle of some rice fields. Battle with the Vietcong was raging. Suddenly in the heat of the battle the soldiers saw six Buddhist monks appear to their right. They started to walk along the raised wooden ledges which separated one paddy field from the next. They were perfectly calm and relaxed as they walked towards the line of fire.

'They didn't look right, they didn't look left. They walked straight through,' recalls David Busch, one of the American soldiers. 'It was really strange, because nobody shot at 'em. And after they walked over the berm (the ledge between the fields), suddenly all the fight was out of me. It just didn't feel like I wanted to do this any more, at least not that day. It must have been that way for everybody, because everybody quit. We just stopped fighting.'

Reflections

- Those six monks affected the course of fighting that day. Their peaceful calm brought the battle to an end. No one had the energy to carry on fighting afterwards. This true story illustrates a simple truth: we all catch our moods from each other. Emotions are contagious.

- We all send emotional signals to one another. We need to take responsibility for the signals we give to each other and be challenged to have a positive influence on all we meet.

- Today let us promise to have a positive impact upon the people we meet.

40. The really important things in life

Theme: Acting with both our head and our heart

Introduction

Psychologists tell us that our brain is divided into two sides. The left side of the brain controls the right side of the body and is concerned with our thinking skills – our ability to be logical. The right side of the brain controls the left side of the body and is responsible for feelings and creativity.

In the technological world in which we live a lot of pressure is put upon us to develop our left-brain activities – to act in logical and analytical ways. We are encouraged to develop our thinking skills. Sometimes we concentrate so much on these skills that we ignore our right-brain activities – our creativity and imagination.

The following reading, taken from Antoine De Saint Exupery's children's novel, The Little Prince, *shows how important it is to live from the heart as well as from the mind.*

Reading

Grown-ups love figures. When you tell them that you have made a new friend, they never ask you any questions about essential matters. They never say to you, 'What does his voice sound like? What games does he love best? Does he collect butterflies?' Instead, they demand, 'How old is he? How many brothers has he? How much does he weigh? How much money does his father make?' Only from these figures do they think they have learned anything about him.

If you were to say to grown-ups, 'I saw a beautiful house made of rosy bricks, with geraniums in the windows and doves on the roof,' they would not be able to get any idea of that house at all. You would have to say to them, 'I saw a house that cost $20,000.' Then they would exclaim, 'Oh, what a pretty house that is!'

(*The Little Prince*, Antoine De Saint Exupery)

Reflections

- Do you think the Little Prince has a point? Do adults really act this way? What does it tell you about adults' values?

- In order to be whole people we need to be aware of both our heart and our minds. We need to live in harmony with ourselves.

41. The teacher who died for his students

Theme: Self-sacrifice

Introduction

It is rare that you meet a person who is willing to lay down their life for other people. It is one thing to think that you might be willing to and another thing to be called upon to do so. The massacre at Columbine High School in April 1999 revealed the courage of one such man: business teacher Dave Sanders. As you read the account of his last hours consider what qualities Dave possessed.

Reading

Dave Sanders gave his all to the students at Columbine High School. On Tuesday 21 April 1999 he gave his life.

The two gunmen, eighteen-year-old Eric Harris and seventeen-year-old Dylan Klebold, had carefully chosen their time to launch their assault. It was 11.40 a.m. and ten minutes into the early lunch break. Over 400 students were packed into the cafeteria. Sanders was outside the lunch room when he saw the gunmen walk towards the corridor. He could have run out of their line of fire. Instead, he burst into the cafeteria giving those present seconds to run to safety. 'He ran into the cafeteria and warned everybody,' English teacher Cheryl Lucas said. 'We started moving because of him.' Together the teachers managed to get most of the children out of the way before the two boys entered to find a virtually empty room.

Sanders then had a choice – to race for safety or else to go and warn others. He chose the second course and in so doing was shot and stumbled into a class where a group of students were hiding. One student recalls, 'Mr Sanders was taking bullets for people. He was a real hero.' As he lay on the floor students tried to stop the bleeding. He lay there for three hours until the siege was over. 'I heard him say, "I'm not going to make it. Tell my girls I love them."'

Sanders was amazing. Instead of thinking about saving his own life he ran everywhere, trying to warn others of the danger. He had a number of opportunities to seek safety. However, he put the students' safety before his own and met his death on that classroom floor.

Reflection

- The greatest love a person can have for his friends is to give his life for them.

(John 15:13)

42. The wicked woman and the onion

Theme: Selfishness

Introduction

Sometimes people have turned in on themselves so much that they find it virtually impossible to be generous towards others. This story is taken from Brothers Karamazov, *a novel by the Russian novelist Fydor Dostoevsky. It shows how people can become so selfish that they destroy themselves.*

Reading

There was once a very wicked woman who died and was taken to the Judgement Seat by the angels. The Judge examined her records but could not find any single act of generosity towards others to save her from the fires of hell.

Her guardian angel took pity on her and asked God whether there was anything that could be done to rescue her. God told the angel that he should search the record of her life carefully to find if she had ever performed any good deed. If he could find one, this could be used to save her.

The angel went away and searched through the Book of Life and, like the Judge, could not find anything to begin with. Eventually, though, he found one kind act. One day a beggar had come to the woman asking for food. She had gone into her garden and pulled up an onion and given it to the beggar.

The angel returned to God and told him this. God then told the angel to go to the lake of fire and lift the woman out, with the help of the onion. The angel went to the lake and called, 'Woman, woman.' She came swimming across the lake of fire and, holding onto the onion, was lifted from the fire. As this happened, others saw what was going on and they grasped hold of the woman's legs in order that they too might be lifted from the lake.

For a moment the woman and a long line of people were being lifted from the lake. But then the wicked woman felt the people tugging on her skirt. She became very angry. 'Off with you, this onion is mine!' Looking down at them, she kicked them away from her and back into the lake of fire. At that moment the onion leaves which were supporting her snapped and she dropped back into the lake.

The angel went away and wept.

(adapted from *The Brothers Karamazov*, Fydor Dostoevsky)

Reflections

- There is a Russian tradition of mothers telling their children that as they go through life they should collect little gold coins that they can show to the Judge at the end of their lives. These gold coins are the good deeds that they perform throughout their lives. Children are taught to build up a bank of these good deeds day by day.

- It is easy to become self-centred. The medicine we need to use to heal ourselves is that of generosity.

43. The work of his life

Theme: The need for self-sacrifice in order to be truly creative in life

Introduction

If you want to achieve anything great in this life it will cost you. Consider the life work of a parent: when parents create a baby they literally put their lives into bringing up their baby. They endure sleepless nights during the first months of the baby's life. This self-sacrifice continues throughout the child's life.

This story comes from Florence, Italy, and illustrates the sacrifices we all need to make in life if we are to live creatively.

Reading

During the sixteenth century a group of artists met together each evening to share their day's work. They discussed new ideas and techniques and supported each other in their work.

One evening one of the painters brought his latest work. He had used a distinctive pigment – a beautiful red which transformed this and all of his following work. His art became popular and people started to pay high prices for it. His friends tried to persuade him to tell them his secret. Which colours did he mix together to get this beautiful red? The painter remained silent, keeping the secret to himself.

One evening he failed to turn up at the tavern. After two days his friends became concerned. They went to his house and knocked on his door, but there was no reply. They had no option but to break the door down. As they entered the friends found the artist's body lying on the floor amidst paintings he was working on. As they examined his body they found an open wound on his left arm. It was then that they discovered the secret pigment that he had been using in his work. He had been using his own blood. He had truly sacrificed his life for art.

Reflections

• To live creatively is a costly business. To create anything great we have to be willing to make personal sacrifices. For example, great athletes, musicians and artists commit themselves to hours of practice each day.

• Consider what you want to achieve in life, and what sacrifices you will have to make in order to achieve it. To achieve results you must be willing to put your life into your work.

• *Remember: If a man hasn't discovered something that he would die for, he isn't fit to live.*
(Martin Luther King Jr, 1929–1968, American civil rights leader)

44. Where are we going to?

Theme: The need to practise tolerance

Introduction

Look at the world around you. What's the world coming to? Every day the news brings us stories of hatred, terrorism and of people starving and being slaughtered as a result of 'ethnic cleansing'. This state of affairs has led some leaders to fear that society is sinking back into a state of barbarism.

This reading describes the dangers of intolerance and the importance of treating each person as of equal worth if we are going to live in harmony with each other.

Reading

Political and religious leaders fear for the state of the world in a week that saw another bomb attack in London – this time on the Admiral Duncan pub in Soho – coupled with the events of the killing of fifteen pupils and staff at Columbine High School in Denver. In the Balkans an ethnic slaughter is going on in Kosovo.

'When I think about what's been going on in America, when you know of what's been going on in Kosovo, we seem to be, at the end of our Millennium, sinking back to a kind of barbarism,' said Cardinal Basil Hume, Archbishop of Westminster. 'It's terrifying, and we really need – as a society – to take a very long look at ourselves as to what values we are giving to our people and how we are bringing up our young.'

(Cardinal Basil Hume, 1923–1999, late Archbishop of Westminster)

The bomb which went off in Soho was directly aimed at the gay community, whilst the 'ethnic cleansing' going on in Kosovo is aimed at a whole race of people. Both incidents draw attention to growing hatred and violence within our society. In a speech to more than 2000 Sikhs in Birmingham, the Prime Minister Tony Blair argued that the whole world must unite to fight intolerance. 'The message of tolerance and respect at the heart of the Sikh faith could not be more relevant at home, where blacks, Asians and gays have been under attack, or in Kosovo where intolerance, bigotry and racial hatred have caused scenes of barbarity not seen in Europe since the Second World War. The recognition that we are of equal worth is why we must fight all forms of discrimination at home and defeat the evil of ethnic cleansing abroad.'

(Tony Blair quoted in *Sunday Telegraph*, 2 May 1999)

Reflections

- Do you think that the world is sinking into barbarism? What signs of hope are there?

- Why do you think people are intolerant of one another?

45. Actions speak louder than words

Theme: Acting on our values

Introduction

We show what values we believe in not by what we say but by what we do. People express their morality by how they act. Therefore it is important that our actions match our words. The way we live our lives bears witness to the values we hold.

Compassion is the ability to feel for someone who is suffering. This poem explains how we need to show our compassion for others in our actions towards them.

Reading

I was hungry –
> And you formed a Humanities club and discussed my hunger...
> Thank you.

I was in prison –
> And you went quietly to your chapel and prayed for my release.

I was naked –
> And in your mind you debated the morality of my appearance.

I was sick –
> And you knelt and thanked God for your health.

I was homeless –
> And you preached to me about the shelter of the love of God.

I was lonely –
> And you left me alone to pray for me.

You seemed so holy, so close to God:
> But I am still very hungry, very cold and very lonely.

(Anonymous)

Reflections

- *Preach the gospel always. Use words if you have to.*
(St Francis of Assisi 1182–1226 CE)

- *Throughout history it has been the inaction of those who could have acted, the indifference of those who should have known better, the silence of the voice of justice when it mattered most, that has made it possible for evil to triumph.*
(Haile Selassie, 1892–1975, Ethiopian emperor)

- *Words that do not match deeds are not important.*
(Che Guevara, 1928–1967, Cuban revolutionary)

- *To see what is right and not to do it is want of courage.*
(*Analects*, Confucius, 551–479 BCE, Chinese philosopher and founder of Confucianism)

- *He who hath compassion upon others receives compassion from Heaven.*
(*Talmud*, c.late fourth to sixth century, ancient body of Jewish civil and canonical law, Shabbat 151)

Part 3

Values for society

46. All right mate! Hey, man!

Theme: Greetings

Introduction

One of the sad facts about modern life is that we all tend to live in our own 'little boxes'. People used to live in small communities – villages and towns – where everyone knew each other. Today it is possible for people to live lonely lives shut in their own homes, sometimes not speaking to a single person for days on end. Sometimes news stories inform us of people who have died in their homes and not been found for weeks. What does this say about modern society?

Do you know the names of each member of the family who lives next door to you? Recent research tells us that 70 per cent of people do not know the name of their next door neighbour. Seventy per cent! People appear to be frightened of getting involved in each others' lives. What can we do to get back in touch with the people we live with?

Reading

How do you greet each other when you meet? What do you say? Do you hug each other, shake each others' hands? What are you saying to each other in the way that you greet them?

In Asia people greet each other not only with words but with their whole bodies. In India, people will stand still, clasp their hands together, smile and look into your eyes and say, 'Namaste!' which means, 'I bow to the Light in You.'

In Central Africa, one person will say to the other, 'I am here to be seen.' The other person will reply, 'I see you.'

These greetings are blessings. They take each person seriously. They recognize the value of the person you are greeting. Each

Values for society

person can become our teacher, teaching us something about life from their own experiences. Are we willing to take each person we meet seriously and learn from them?

Reflections

- In groups, invent your own greeting which can act as a blessing. It should point to the unique worth of each person. Try it out when you meet people over the next week.

- Remember today, you are in great company. Everyone you meet can hold a gift for you. They can be your teachers.

47. The merchant of death

Theme: Contributing to society

Introduction

Have you ever thought what it would be like to pick up the newspaper one morning and read about your own death? Today's reading tells the story of one man who did just that. What he read in the morning newspaper completely changed his life from that moment onwards.

Reading

It happened just over a hundred years ago. A famous scientist came down to breakfast and, as was his custom, he picked up the morning newspaper. On the front page he saw his own death reported. They had made a mistake, but he couldn't resist turning the pages to find what they had written about him.

The title reported, 'Dynamite king dies'. The text went on to record how he was an accomplished chemist by the time he was sixteen, and was fluent in German, French, Russian and Swedish. After receiving an education in St Petersburg, Russia and in the United States, he returned to Russia to work for his father developing mines, torpedoes and other explosives. He became famous for the manufacture of the liquid explosive nitroglycerin. However, shortly after this invention there occurred a tragic mistake. His factory blew up, causing the death of his youngest brother and four other people.

As he read on he was startled to find himself described as 'a merchant of death'. He had invented dynamite and had become very rich by the production of weapons of mass destruction. He was shocked that after his death he would be remembered as the 'merchant of death'. From that moment on he resolved to dedicate the remainder of his life to working for peace. He left

Values for society

the bulk of his massive fortune to a trust to establish what came to be the most highly regarded of international rewards: the Nobel Prize. His name was Alfred Bernhard Nobel (1833–1896).

Reflections

• What do you want to be remembered for? Try writing the qualities you want people to remember you for.

• What sort of person would you like to be? We all have the ability to change who we are. All we need is the belief and determination that 'I can change'.

48. A question of integrity

Theme: Should the leader of a country provide moral leadership?

Introduction

Do you expect your country's leaders to be squeaky clean? What do you think should happen to political leaders who make personal mistakes?

This debate has been going on down the centuries. The Greek philosopher Plato (c.428–347 BCE) taught that people who are to be leaders should undergo years of moral training before they took political power, and once in power they should set an example for people to live by. Others believe that their leaders are only human and that their personal lives have little connection with their public lives.

This debate about a public person's private life became the topic of worldwide discussion when, in 1999, President Clinton was tried by the Senate for something he had done in his private life. This reading explores the issues.

Reading

In 1999 the President of the United States, Bill Clinton, faced a trial by the Senate for mistakes made in his personal life. President Clinton at first lied about his affair with Monica Lewinsky. When Tony Blair, the British Prime Minister, was asked whether it mattered what politicians did in their private lives he commented that affairs did not make men unfit for office. 'Bill Clinton ... has always conducted himself with strength, determination and integrity.'

(Tony Blair quoted in the *Daily Telegraph*, 6 February 1998)

Consider the responses of ordinary citizens to the President's affair.

Values for society

My problem with President Clinton is not that he's shown he is human; it is the fact that he is a fraud and a hypocrite.

(Ed Cunion, Johannesburg, quoted in *TIME Magazine*, 28 September 1998)

I just can't see him ever having any credibility with any foreign leaders.

(Lowell Davis, quoted in *The Times*, 12 September 1998)

Let us judge President Bill Clinton according to Abraham Lincoln's job description for the presidency of the United States: 'Government of the people, by the people, for the people.'

On the first and third counts, Mr Clinton's performance is beyond dispute. No other president has enjoyed as earnest a debate with the American people, and under his watch, the wealth of the average American has steadily increased.

What the Monica Lewinsky matter has shown us is that this president is neither a saint nor a criminal; in truth he is just one of us. That is a clear case of government 'by' the people.

Three out of three isn't bad.

Emile Servan-Schreiber, Neuilly-sur-Seine, France. Letter in *International Herald Tribune*, 1 October 1998)

Reflections

- Do you think the private lives of politicians affect their ability to do their jobs?

- Integrity means that a person's actions and values are consistent; in other words, a person acts as they believe. If public figures lack integrity in their private life how do you know that they are showing integrity in their public duties?

- The Greek philosopher Socrates (c.470–399 BCE) believed that to live a life of shame is to live a life that is not worth living. Here is one description of integrity: 'It takes a long time to make a good glass vase. It only takes a second to break it and a long time to put it back together again.' A person's integrity is tested under pressure. What worth is integrity when I can gain from giving in?

- *Governors must never forget that he who is unable to run his own house and family is still less competent to be entrusted with public matters.*

  (Pachacutec Inca Yupanqui, 1438–1471, Incan ruler)

- What is to prevent us from turning into the kind of person we don't respect?

49. More equals less

Theme: The dangers of materialism

Introduction

In the first year of its existence the National Lottery made 102 people millionaires. Twenty people each won over 5 million pounds. However, there is only a fourteen million to one chance that you will win a fortune if you play. So why do people continue to play? What are they seeking?

Some would argue that they are seeking happiness: if only they won the lottery they would live happily ever after. But is this the case? Research indicates otherwise.

In recent years, more than five hundred extensive pieces of psychology research have shown quite conclusively that, since the 1950s, (1) we have more things and more wealth than ever before; (2) we are more depressed, more violent, more suicidal and more stressed than ever before. The research indicates that 'more equals less', i.e. as we acquire more we become more demanding and less satisfied.

(*Happiness Now!*, Robert Holden)

This reading is the story of the first person to win a fortune on the Lottery. It illustrates that more money does not necessarily equal more happiness.

Reading

18m Family Lottery Winner – HAND IT BACK

The family of the dad-of-three who scooped the £18 million lottery jackpot begged him to give it back today. Relatives of the Indian born factory worker said, 'The pressure is enormous.' Not just for him, but for all of us in Blackburn ... Last night, as he planned to flee Britain with his 33-year-old wife and sons, another relative said, 'He's in a terrible state. He's beginning to think he'd be better off if he'd just won a few pounds.' He has told relatives, 'This had made my life a nightmare.'

(*Daily Star*, 15 December 1994)

Reflections

- In what ways can money ruin a person's life? Why do you think the Lottery winner said that winning had made life a nightmare for him?

- *The love of money causes all kinds of evil.*

  (1 Timothy 6:10)

  Do you agree?

- The more some people have the less they feel that they can give away.

- Be careful not to wrap your identity in possessions.

- *Lust for fame and fortune is like an intoxication. While a man is intoxicated, he doesn't realize it. It's only after it is all over that he realizes that everything is like an illusion. If men could realize this all the time, there would be much less trouble on earth, and there would be much happier people too.*

  (*Ching-hua yuan, Flowers in the Mirror*, Li Ju-chen, c. 1763–1830, Chinese writer)

50. Three kids = a nightmare

Theme: The generation gap

Introduction

The term 'generation gap' is used to describe the differences in attitude and opinion between different generations. It is often given as a reason for the lack of understanding which both parents and children sometimes feel for each other.

Today's reading is a real letter submitted to the tax office by a father. In it he humorously – but also seriously – describes his relationship with his three children.

Reading

Dear Sirs,

I am responding to your letter denying the deduction for two of the three dependents that I claimed on my 1994 Tax Return. Thank you. I have questioned whether or not these are my children for years. They are evil and expensive. It's only fair that since they are under the legal age, but not my responsibility, the government (who evidently is taxing me more to care for these waifs) knows something about them and what to expect over the next year.

The oldest, Kristen, is now seventeen. She is brilliant. Ask her! I suggest you put her to work in your office where she can answer people's questions about their tax returns. While she has no formal training, it has not seemed to hamper her giving knowledgeable opinions on any other subject you can name. Taxes should be a breeze. Next year she is going to college. I think it's wonderful that you will now be responsible for that little expense. While you mull that over keep in mind that she

Values for society

has a boyfriend. Oh joy! While she possesses all the wisdom of the universe, her alleged mother and I have felt it best occasionally to remind her of the virtues of abstinence and – in the face of overwhelming passion – safe sex. This topic is always uncomfortable and I am quite relieved you will be handling it in the future.

Patrick is fourteen. I've had my suspicions about this one. His eyes are a little close together for normal people. In February I was awakened at three in the morning by a police officer who was bringing Pat home. Kids at fourteen will do almost anything for a dare. His hair is purple. Permanent dye, temporary dye, what's the big deal? Learn to deal with it. You'll have plenty of time as he is sitting out a few days of school after instigating a food fight. I'll take care of filing your phone number with the Deputy Head. Oh yes, he and all of his friends have raging hormones. This – the house of testosterone – will be much more peaceful when he lives in your home. DO NOT leave any of them unsupervised with girls, explosives, inflammables, inflatables, vehicles or telephones.

Heather is an alien. She slid through a time warp and appeared quite by magic one year. I'm sure this one is yours. She is ten going on twenty-one. She wears tie-dyed clothes, beads, sandals and hair that looks like Tiny Tim's. It's quite obvious that we were terrible parents (ask the other two) so they have helped raise this one to a new level of terror. She cannot speak English. Most people under twenty understand the curious patois she has fashioned out of reggae–yuppie–political doublespeak. I don't. She wears hats backwards, pants baggy and wants one of her ears pierced four more times. She has a fascination with tattoos that worries me but I am sure that you can handle it. Bring a truck when you come to get her, as she sort of 'nests' in her room and I think that it would be easier to move the entire thing than find out what it is really made of.

You denied two of the three exemptions so it is only fair you get to pick which two you will take. I prefer that you take the youngest, I'll still go bankrupt with Kristen's college fees but then

Values for society

I am free! If you take the two oldest then I still have time for counselling before Heather becomes a teenager. If you take the two girls then I won't feel so bad about putting Patrick in a military academy.

Yours Truly,

Bob

Reflections

- With whom do you identify in this story – if anyone?

- Do you experience a generation gap in your family? What are the issues? How best do you deal with them?

- Do you think a generation gap between parents and children is inevitable?

51. School for bullies

Theme: Bullying

Introduction

When people mention bullying, many of us automatically think of it taking place in school. However, bullies don't just exist in the school playground. They exist in all walks of life. Sometimes it is the boss who bullies employees, at other times colleagues at work. Bullying is responsible for 30–50 per cent of stress-related illnesses at work. Bullying forms a large part of domestic abuse at home. It can take the form of verbal abuse or emotional abuse as well as physical abuse.

According to a study undertaken at Keele University in 1997, more than 80 per cent of secondary-school pupils are involved in some degree of bullying, either as victims or perpetrators. In the last few years the tragic results of bullying at school have been highlighted by a number of young people who have taken their own lives because they have been scared and frightened of going to school. It is believed that bullying leads to as many as twelve suicides a year. This reading tells of one such suicide.

Reading

In May 1999 a twelve-year-old girl, Natalie Smith, was found on her grandmother's bathroom floor after taking 100 painkillers. She had become so miserable, after being tormented by bullies at school, that she could see no other way out.

The bullying began at the beginning of the school year, when two girls at school took a £200 jacket belonging to her sister. At first, Natalie was befriended by the girls who then took advantage of her, making her hand over money and searching her to make sure that she wasn't hiding any. When she refused to give them things they punched her in the face and kicked her.

On the night before she took her own life she contacted all her relatives to say goodbye.

Values for society

Reflections

- How can people – working together – stop bullying?

- *Bullies are not special, not strong, not tough. In fact they usually need to appear powerful because they secretly feel weak.*

    (*A Streetwise Guide to Coping with Bullying*,
    Metropolitan Police Service)

Do you agree?

52. Drivers behaving badly

Theme: Road rage

Introduction

Have you ever become annoyed with other drivers on the road? What upsets you most?

Sometimes people become so upset on the roads that they act out their aggression towards other drivers and their cars. Over the last few years roads have become hijacked by tarmac terrorists: drivers who become openly violent when they are behind the wheel and are even willing to go to desperate lengths to get their revenge. The concept of 'road rage' may be relatively new but this form of violence has already cost hundreds of lives. The term has become increasingly used by the police and the press in Britain since 1994.

Road rage has become such a common phenomenon that it now appears in the Oxford English Dictionary. Road rage is 'violent anger caused by the stress and frustration of driving a motor vehicle; especially an act of violence committed by one motorist against another, provoked by the supposedly objectionable driving of the victim.'

This reading asks who these tarmac terrorists are, and what causes them to become so aggressive behind a car's wheel.

Reading

The AA found that 90 per cent of motorists have been victims of road rage and that 60 per cent admitted losing their temper while driving. Road rage can take many forms, ranging from gestures and verbal abuse to physical attacks. According to the annual Lex Report on Motoring, some 500,000 people have had their cars deliberately driven into and 250,000 people have been attacked by other drivers. Thousands of people have been forced off the road.

Values for society

Activities that have upset drivers include honking of the horn, cutting people up when overtaking, speeding in towns and cities, overtaking on the inside lane, cruising in the middle and outside lane on motorways, stealing a parking space, using a mobile phone and not concentrating on the road ahead. The violence has led to a number of tragedies.

- A sixteen-month-old girl died when her father's car was forced off the road by another motorist.

- Days before that, Peter Swales, 39, was beaten to death after an argument with the driver of another car.

- A driver, cross about being 'cut up', chased the other car at speeds of up to 80 miles per hour before crashing into oncoming traffic, leaving three people dead.

- A grandfather died of a heart attack at the wheel of his car after being harassed and abused by a van driver.

- In America road rage has become so common that over a five-year period 218 people were killed as a result of violence on the road, and a further 12,000 injured.

So what causes people to lose their tempers when they get behind the wheel? A number of reasons have been put forward. Firstly, people are in a hurry to get from A to B. They feel the pressure of a busy lifestyle and take out their stress on other drivers. Secondly, the roads are becoming more crowded, leading to frustration and impatience.

Thirdly, some would argue that society is becoming more violent. In all areas of life people are showing less courtesy to each other and, instead, are using obscene gestures and swearwords. Fourthly, it has been argued that when a person is in a car they become masters of the vehicle. They see other cars as mere lumps of metal. They dehumanize other drivers and turn them into their enemies who are stopping them from getting to their next appointment.

Advice to drivers on how to prevent road rage:

- Allow plenty of time for your journey so that you reduce the chance of frustrations affecting you.

- Avoid driving too close to the car in front of you.

- If you make a mistake, gesture an apology to the other driver.

- If someone is driving badly do not get involved. It is not your job to teach them a lesson.

Reflections

- Some people suggest that those who are violent on the road need counselling to control their aggression. What do you think is an appropriate treatment?

- It's all a matter of attitude. You have the ability to decide how you are going to react in any given situation. Be courteous to others, don't rise to the bait.

- *You're either part of the problem or part of the solution.*
  (*Soul on Ice*, Eldridge Cleaver)

53. Living 'inside' television

Theme: A critical look at the influence of the media in society

Introduction

Where do you get your ideas from? How much influence do television and videos have on you in forming your ideas? Has television ever changed your mind on an issue?

How many hours of television and videos do you watch each week? Keep a time check for the next week. What do the results tell you about the importance of television in your life? What would your life be like if you did not have a television?

This reading examines both the positive and negative effect which television has on people's lives.

Reading

The media are all around us – newspapers, magazines, television, videos, the Internet. They have a powerful influence on our lives today. Just how powerful the media can be was demonstrated by the way the Nazis used it to manipulate hatred towards the Jews in the 1930s and 1940s. They used the media to turn a whole nation against the Jewish people. This resulted in the extermination of over six million Jews in the Holocaust.

A survey in 1991 found out that, on average, children spend 21 hours per week watching television. The same survey discovered that on average fathers spend 25 minutes per week (3.5 minutes per day) and mothers spend 38 minutes per week (5.5 minutes per day) in genuine conversation with their child or children. It is clear that the television has a big influence in shaping the ideas of today's young people.

Values for society

One researcher into the effects of the media makes the following point.

Consider the power of television, and the millions of people who live ... inside television ... Television has become the physical universe that people now relate to, and the mental universe as well ... Millions live off the same television images.
(Brenda Lealman, 'The whole vision of the child' in *Education, Spirituality and the Whole Child*, R. Best)

The Dalai Lama, the spiritual and political leader of the exiled Tibetans, speaks of both the positive and negative effects which the media can have.

Now for the media. I respect them very much and I appreciate the fact that they interfere with everyone's business! From time to time some public figures might abuse their position, showing neither moral principles nor self-discipline. There should be no discrepancy between the external appearance and the inner life of an honest person. In such cases, I think the media alone have the power to verify and expose such behaviour. Journalists are notoriously nosy and do their job well. (Furthermore) I think that if we did not expose all the evils of society, such as drugs, murder, sexual abuse and exploitation of children, innocent people would still continue to suffer from them daily. On the other hand, I reproach them for attaching too much importance to the negative aspects which can greatly discourage the human mind.
(*Beyond Dogma: the challenge of the modern world*, Dalai Lama)

Values for society

Reflections

- What do you think Brenda Lealman means when she says 'Millions live off the same television images'?

- In what ways do you think the media can be both positive and negative? Do you agree with the Dalai Lama that journalists have a responsibility for researching into the private lives of important people?

- The television has a large part to play in shaping a person's view of life, their ideas of what is right and what is wrong. In a way the television acts as our teacher. But what values is television promoting?

- No one doubts that TV is immensely powerful in today's society. However, people have different views on its power. Discuss one of the following statements:

  Violence on TV makes people more violent.

  Advertisers are convinced that advertisements change our buying habits.

  TV does not make our moral values, all it does is mirror what is going on in society.

  Sexually explicit scenes should only be screened after nine o'clock.

  Video age ratings are a joke.

54. Trained to kill

Theme: Violence in the media

Introduction

Do you watch violent films, or play with interactive video and computer games which contain violence? If so, why? What effect do you think violence on TV has? Do you think it encourages young people to become violent?

In 1998 almost 1200 scenes involving guns and 798 violent assaults were featured in just 269 films screened on terrestrial channels. These films also contained 107 arson or bombing attacks, 340 attacks with knives or other weapons and 44 scenes involving illegal drugs. Is this just entertainment or does it have a more serious effect?

This decade has seen an increase in violent crime amongst the young. So from where do young people get their violent ideas?

15 years after the introduction of TV, homicides, rapes and assaults doubled in the United States.

(American Medical Association, quoted in *Christianity Today*)

Today's reading describes a piece of research which suggests how television can condition people to become more violent.

Reading

David Grossman is a military expert on the psychology of killing. He believes that today's media is training children to kill.

Killing requires training because there is an in-built aversion to killing one's own kind. It does not come naturally. You have to be taught to kill. Children don't naturally kill; they learn it from violence in the home and most pervasively, from violence as entertainment in television, movies, and interactive games.

(David Grossman, quoted in *Christianity Today*)

Values for society

Grossman believes that the media teach young people to become violent in the following three ways:

1. *By desensitizing children to violence*: children watch television from an early age. They slowly become desensitized to all the violence they see and treat it as normal. *The Journal of the American Medical Association* has published evidence of what happens to a society once the TV, and TV violence, is introduced. 'In every nation, region, or city with television, there is an immediate explosion of violence on the playground, and within fifteen years there is a doubling of the murder rate. Why fifteen years? That is how long it takes for the brutalization of a three-to-five year old to reach the "prime crime age". Today the data linking violence in the media to violence in society are superior to those linking cancer and tobacco. Hundreds of sound scientific studies demonstrate the social impact of brutalization by the media.'

2. *By conditioning children to act in a certain way*: because children watch so much television violence they no longer become affected by it. Instead, they associate such films with pleasure and carry on eating their popcorn and drinking pop! 'We have raised a generation of barbarians who have learned to associate violence with pleasure. The result is a phenomenon that functions much like AIDS, which I call AVIDS – Acquired Violence Immune Deficiency Syndrome. AIDS has never killed anybody. It destroys your immune system, and then other diseases that shouldn't kill you become fatal. Television violence by itself does not kill you. It destroys your violence immune system and conditions you to derive pleasure from violence.'

3. *By operant conditioning*: this acts like programming so that when you are in a situation you act out of reflex. In the army soldiers are trained to shoot as soon as they see the enemy. So also with the video and computer games children play.

They are developing a reflex reaction to shoot the enemy. Children are developing violent habits.

Reflections

- *Few researchers bother any longer to dispute that bloodshed on TV and in the movies has an effect on kids who witness it.*
(*TIME Magazine*, 6 April 1998)

  Do you agree with the researchers?

- When you watch TV this week monitor the amount of violence you see – it could be on news programmes, documentaries or films. Be aware of the different types of violence: domestic violence in the home, violence between different groups in society and violence between countries.

- The average child gets more one-to-one communication from TV than from all her parents and teachers combined.

  Do you agree? What impact do you think the TV has?

- What can be done to combat all the TV violence? Should the law legislate against it? Are TV producers acting responsibly? If you had children would you censor what they watch on TV? Is this practical or realistic?

55. A high school massacre

Theme: Teenage violence – what is the world coming to?

Introduction

Sometimes a story hits the news and shocks the world. One such story started to take shape soon after 11 a.m. on Tuesday 20 April 1999, as two high-school students turned their school into a killing ground. Four hours later fifteen people were dead and sixteen were injured. The shooting was the latest in a series of incidents at schools across the United States. People all over the world asked the same question, 'Why, why, why?'

Reading

On Tuesday 20 April 1999 two members of the Trenchcoat Mafia gang chose the 110th anniversary of Hitler's birth to slaughter their classmates with bullets and bombs. The day before had been the anniversary of the siege at Waco and the Oklahoma City bombing. At 8.41 a.m. that fateful Tuesday morning one of the two killers, eighteen-year-old Eric Harris, logged onto his computer and posted a message on the Internet: 'Today is my last day on earth. Be prepared.'

The bloodiest school shooting in history began at about 11.40 a.m. as Eric Harris and Dylan Klebold, seventeen, wearing their trademark black trenchcoats, entered the school and started shooting with sub-machine guns. Witnesses said the gunmen fired randomly and set off explosives, laughing as they went. About 400 pupils eating an early lunch in the ground-floor cafeteria mistook the popping sounds from outside as a prank. Seconds later Dave Saunders, a popular business teacher, burst into the cafeteria. He was shouting, 'Get under the tables, get down.' Panic erupted. Students fled into the car park and ran for safety. When Harris and Klebold ran through the doors the dining room was virtually empty. Saunders was shot.

The gunmen then proceeded calmly upstairs to the library, where they found 45 students hiding under desks that were to provide little shelter. 'There was a girl crouched under a desk, and one of the gunmen came over and said, "Peekaboo!" and shot her in the neck,' said Bryon Kirkland, fifteen, who escaped uninjured. Altogether nine students were shot dead in the library before the two boys moved onto classrooms to terrorize classes locked behind doors.

Police arrived at the school within five minutes of the first shooting. However, they feared to enter because of the number of bombs and booby traps which the gunmen had placed all over the school. During the siege fifteen explosions were heard. Police discovered a further 30 devices during the afternoon. The siege ended when Harris and Klebold rigged explosives to their bodies and each shot themselves in the head. The shots were fired at 12.30 p.m. The massacre had lasted an hour.

That was not the end of the story. Within days of the massacre 'copycats' emerged. In Colorado Springs four teenagers arrived at school wearing trenchcoats and masks. In Ohio a thirteen-year-old boy was taken into police custody after he threatened to shoot all the people he did not like in the school. Five fourteen-year-olds in Texas were detained after making plans to assassinate teachers and students.

Reflections

• Could a similar shooting happen in your school? What happens in the minds of young people, that they can think of carrying out such a massacre?

• In the days after the massacre the Internet was flooded with people's responses. Here are a few of them. Do you agree with any of them?

Values for society

The reason for so many school shootings this past year is because, for one thing, parents don't discipline their kids well and they don't teach them right from wrong.

(Erin, Virginia)

If we want this killing to stop we have to get rid of the guns. Ever since this happened I am now petrified to go to school because I wonder if someone will come and start killing off people in my school.

(Christina, fifteen, Canada)

There are no simple solutions. But I do know that making it easy for kids to get guns and build bombs, and filling their minds with media images and lyrics that glorify and sensationalize violence and murder, will make these tragedies all the more frequent and inevitable. I strongly believe that if we don't want to live in a violent society then as a society we have to stop glorifying violence.

(Victoria)

- Do you think our society glorifies violence? If so, how?

144

56. Revenge of the trenchcoat misfits

Theme: Outcasts and misfits

Introduction

Eric Harris and Dylan Klebold will be remembered in years to come for the massacre they reeked in their own school, killing fifteen classmates and injuring sixteen more. On Tuesday 20 April 1999 they went on a rampage at their school. What led them to such a terrible crime?

As journalists researched their lives they discovered the story of two boys who felt rejected by their peers. They became known as outcasts and misfits, and faced ridicule from their fellow students. They resorted to violence to resolve their problems and seek their revenge. What lessons can we learn from their tragic tale? Who is to blame for what happened on that April day in 1999?

The following reading traces the background of these two boys in the hope of providing some clues as to why they carried out this terrible crime.

Reading

People who knew Eric Harris, eighteen, when he lived in upstate New York, remember a middle-class boy who was interested in the usual teenage things. He was a baseball fan and enjoyed playing basketball with his elder brother Daniel. Before he moved to the city he had close friends and girlfriends. He didn't stand out from the crowd. The only thing Harris disliked was failure.

In 1996 his family moved into the affluent suburb of Littleton, Colorado. Eric became a pupil at Columbine High School where the motto is 'Stretch for excellence'. It is one of eight schools designated as World Class in the US and Canada. For a boy who loved games, the competitive atmosphere of the school became a threat. At Columbine Eric was good but not special. He also felt a misfit and not really accepted by his peers. Soon after arriving he was dumped by Tiffany Typher, a girl he had been seeing. He took the rejection badly.

Dylan Klebold, seventeen, also came from a middle-class family. He drove a black BMW, one of his parents' seven cars, and was also a big baseball fan. He was a natural ally of Eric. Both were keen on playing sports, but hated to lose. They both came to hate the school's athletes, or 'jocks', as they were called. Both Dylan and Eric dropped out of school sports and spent a lot of their time on the Internet. They became obsessed with computer games, many of them violent. They held computer 'death matches' which went on for hours. In school they became part of a gang of outcasts, called the Trenchcoat Mafia.

The Trenchcoat Mafia gang wore black leather trenchcoats to school whatever the weather – sun or rain. Some of the gang also wore steel-capped boots and Nazi swastikas. The 'jocks' treated the Trenchcoats as a joke. They were the subjects of threats and verbal abuse. As Eric and Dylan became more and more separated from the rest of the kids at school, they clung closer together. They used to spend hours on the Internet visiting neo-Nazi sites. Things started to get more serious in January 1998 when Harris and Klebold stole £300 of electronic equipment from a van. They were caught and punished, being assigned 'anger management' classes to attend. They graduated from these classes with glowing reports.

However, from that point onwards they started planning a massacre. Their diaries show that they were planning it for nearly a year. They even chose the date, 20 April 1999. There was a single entry for that date: 'It's rock and roll time.' During school they made violent videos. One of these showed them wearing trenchcoats and killing the 'jocks'. On the Saturday before the killings they both attended a school dance, dressed smartly in black ties. The police suspect that they used this opportunity to plant homemade bombs all over the school.

Eric and Dylan's lives ended when they shot themselves in the head at 12.30 p.m. on that Tuesday.

Reflections

- Brooks Brown, one of Harris's best friends, told the *Denver Post*, 'He was going after jocks. He hated them with a passion, because they always made fun of him and they always threatened him.' Why did Eric and Dylan feel the need to seek revenge? How could this incident have been prevented?

- Should the school take responsibility for not setting adequate boundaries? Should the staff at Columbine High School have questioned the boys' style of dress, the videos they were making and the messages on the Internet?

- What responsibility do parents have? Should they have known what was going on, what their children were planning?

57. Stone soup

Theme: Commitment to active citizenship – learning to help each other

Introduction

The great seventeenth-century English poet, John Donne (1572–1631) wrote, 'No man is an island, entire of itself; every man is a piece of the continent, a part of the main ... any man's death diminishes me, because I am involved in mankind.'

Television brings the events of the world into our homes. It is easy today to see how we are all part of one world, that we all belong to one another. As one African proverb puts it, 'Together, we find the way.' As global citizens we have a responsibility to become informed about our brothers and sisters in different parts of the world and to discover ways of working together.

The following folktale is about the importance of working together and illustrates that it is by co-operating with each other that we can all benefit.

Reading

Late at night an old woman was awoken by a stranger knocking on her door. She went downstairs and found a tired man asking for something to eat. 'I am sorry,' she said, 'I have nothing to give you. I haven't had any food for days.' So the man went to the house next door. A young man answered, 'I am sorry we haven't had any food for weeks.' Wherever he went throughout the village he was told the same thing. Nobody had any food. 'That's okay,' he said to the woman in one house, 'but do you have a large cooking pot? I have a soup stone in my bag? If you can give me a pot I can make some delicious stone soup.'

The man then took the pot and filled it with water from the river. He put five large stones in the bottom of the pot and lit a fire underneath it. As the pot began to boil, the entire village came out of their houses, curious to watch what he was doing. When the soup had boiled he took a spoon and tasted a mouthful. 'Delicious,' he exclaimed. 'All it needs is a little salt to bring out the flavour of the stones.' 'I will get you some,' shouted a little boy, anxious to have a taste of this unusual soup. He ran off but in seconds was back with the salt.

'Wonderful,' the man said as he again tasted the soup. 'It would be even better if we only had a few potatoes to put in it.' 'I have some potatoes in my kitchen,' shouted one villager. Within moments the soup contained stones, salt and potatoes. 'Excellent,' he said. 'If we only had some meat, this would become a really tasty stew.' Another neighbour rushed home to bring some meat, which the man proceeded to add to the soup. One by one all the villagers brought something to add to the soup – cabbage, leeks, carrots, onions. They all wanted to have a taste of the stone soup.

When everybody had contributed the man spoke. 'Thank you very much, but there's far too much for me to eat by myself. Everybody must help themselves.' So they all brought their bowls. This was the first meal that the whole village had shared together. Everyone agreed that this stone soup was the tastiest that they had ever had. Whilst everyone was tucking in to the delicious soup the man quietly slipped away to continue on his journey.

Reflections

- The world can easily be divided into the 'haves' and 'have-nots'. In what ways would our society be different if people acted on the message of the stone soup folktale? Is the idea only fanciful, or is it practical?

Values for society

- *There is no escape – man drags man down, or man lifts man up.*

  (Booker T. Washington, 1856–1915, American educator)

- *Earth provides enough to satisfy every man's need, but not every man's greed.*

  (*Small is Beautiful*, Mohandas K. Gandhi)

58. Making a difference

Theme: Building a better world

Introduction

It is sometimes easy to think that, because individually we are so small and insignificant, we can't really change much in the world. The following reading shows, however, that with a little imagination and goodwill we can all make the world a better place, one day at a time. We each have the power to give, and encourage others to join us in building a better world that works for everyone. Greatness grows out of a simple act of giving.

Reading

Many of us buy cosmetics and soaps from The Body Shop, but how many of us are aware that all the staff who work there are allowed paid time off – half a day a month – to help out in community projects? Some choose to take part in environmental projects, others in animal welfare, and yet others in caring for elderly people.

Some staff participate in international programmes. One of these projects takes place in Romania. It all started in 1990 when the television news covered the tragedies happening there. For the last 26 years the people had suffered under the dictatorship of Nicolae Ceausecu. The country had been left in ruins, with thousands of babies orphaned in horrific conditions. Anita Roddick, the founder of The Body Shop, made a trip to Romania to see what was happening for herself. 'I was horrified by what I saw. The horror filled my thoughts for weeks.'

On her return home she set up the Romanian Relief Drive. Staff from her shops volunteered to go out there and help refurbish the orphanages, cuddle babies with AIDS and give them something many had never had before – love and care. It is now called the Eastern Europe Relief Drive and is run by a handful of

Values for society

young staff members who save up their half-days to contribute to society.

Anita Roddick comments, 'Their desire to help out has been shared by over 450 members of our staff from around the world, who have been out to work as volunteers. The staff come back changed people. Their values suddenly take a leap into a previously unknown source of power for them. They start dreaming of noble purposes.'

Reflections

- Why do you think Anita Roddick pays for her staff to spend time giving to others? What do you think the employees get from helping in this way? Do you think other companies would benefit from this?

- This story shows what can happen when just a few people decide to make a difference. How could you make a difference?

- *Everyone can be great because everyone can serve.*
  (Martin Luther King Jr, 1929–1968, American civil rights leader)

- Each and every one of us can become an everyday hero.

- *If you think you are too small to be effective you have never been in bed with a mosquito.*
  (Bette Reese)

- *Love thy neighbour as thyself because you are your neighbour.*
  (Sarvepalli Radhakrishnan, 1888–1975,
  President of India 1962–1967)

59. The rainbow people

Theme: Equality and diversity in our multi-cultural society

Introduction

During the 1960s blacks struggled for equal rights in the civil rights movement. Although today black people hold positions of authority, recent events have drawn our attention to the fact that racism is still rampant in society.

In 1999 the British Government recognized that 'institutional racism' existed, not only in the police force but in many organizations in British public life, and promised to fight it wherever it was to be found. This story explores why people are racist.

Reading

At the top of the hill lived the Blues. They wore blue clothes, lived in blue homes, drove blue cars and believed that God was blue. At the bottom of the mountain, in a beautiful green valley, lived the Greens. They always wore green clothes, lived in green houses, drove green cars and believed that God was green.

Each group of people was taught that the other group was bad. Green parents would teach their children to say:

Green is happy;
Blue is sad.
Greens are good;
Blues are bad.

The two groups were so afraid of each other that they went out of their way not to mix. Some people lived the whole of their lives without ever coming into contact with people from the other group.

Values for society

It so happened that one day, as he went to play in the meadow, a Green boy saw a Blue boy playing with his kite on Green ground. The Blue boy became frightened at being caught on the enemy territory. He ran, but in his flight he fell and twisted his ankle. Although something in the Green boy wanted to help he didn't dare – after all, his parents had taught him that Blues were bad people.

A few weeks later the Green boy took his dog out for a run. He chased his dog so far that he wasn't aware that he had strayed into Blue territory. Suddenly his dog jumped down some rocks. The Green boy followed but, as he fell, he caught his leg on the branch of a tree and came to the ground with a crash. He yelled for help but he was far from anywhere. As the sunlight faded someone approached the trapped Green boy. It was a Blue. It was the same boy who had sprained his ankle. The Green boy closed his eyes, waiting to be hurt by the Blue. But instead of hurting his enemy the Blue boy broke a branch off the tree and used it as a splint. He tore his blue shirt so that he could tie the branch to the Green boy's leg. Then he helped the Green boy walk home.

When the Green boy's father saw his son's leg tied with the blue cloth he was furious. 'I don't care if you were injured,' he screamed. 'You shouldn't have let a Blue touch you.' Though the Green boy knew that his father was upset he could not forget the Blue boy who had helped him. When his leg healed he went in search of his helper. Going into the Blue neighbourhood took a lot of courage. Everywhere he went doors were slammed on him and young children threw rocks. Finally, he found the boy who had helped him. He was surprised to see that his helper wore a combination of blue and green.

'I thought you learned that green was bad. Why are you wearing green with your blue?' asked the Green boy. 'Do you remember when I helped you? I tore up my blue shirt to make a splint for your leg. I figured that you became part of me, and I became part of you. In helping you and talking with you, I came to see that green is as good as blue.'

Values for society

The two boys became close friends. Gradually the Blues and Greens started visiting each other. Then they started going to each other's schools, and eventually even wandered into the lands of the Reds and the Yellows. After a while most people didn't call themselves 'Greens' or 'Blues', but simply 'Rainbow People'. To this day their children sing, 'There is no colour that is bad.'

(adapted from *Parables for Little People*, Lawrence Castagnola)

Reflections

- Do you think racism is rampant in today's society? If so, what has caused it? The story suggests that racism arises out of people's fear. Do you think this is a good explanation?

- What can be done to break down barriers between people of different races?

- Archbishop Desmond Tutu first used the title 'Rainbow People of God', in a sermon at St George's Cathedral, Cape Town, to describe his hope for a new South Africa post-apartheid. Is this a good way of describing the multi-cultural society in which we live?

- *I have a dream that my four little children will one day live in a nation where they will not be judged by the colour of their skin but by the content of their character.*
  (Martin Luther King Jr, 1929–1968, American civil rights leader, speech in Washington DC, 15 June 1963)

- *The Jewish vision of the world to come is where peace is established between people.*
  (Peah 1:1)

60. The rabbi's son and the holy man who lived just one day away

Theme: One world – setting up barriers between people

Introduction

Sometimes we are so set in our own ways that we do not allow other people and their different viewpoints into our lives. It is tempting to think that only our way is right and that other people's ways are wrong. However, there is great danger in setting up such barriers between people, as the following story illustrates.

Reading

Narrator: Not long ago there lived a rabbi called Nachman of Bratzlaw. He was so studious that he wouldn't even lift his head up to heaven without first checking his holy books to see whether it was the right time to do so. There was nothing that made him so angry as the practices of the Hassids – Jews who celebrated their religion by song and dance. Rabbi Nachman believed they were agents of the evil one, as they broke the peace of the Sabbath with their party-making.

The rabbi eagerly desired a son who would keep his study of the law alive once he had gone. When, as an old man, he was granted a son, he took it as a sign from heaven that his dynasty of learning would be preserved. His son grew very learned, studying night and day. He sat on a tall stool looking out of the window. Now and then he would lift his eyes and watch the birds fly. His heart yearned to become part of this bigger world. But he disciplined himself to carry out his father's commands and thus returned to the holy books.

As time passed, however, the rabbi's son began to look very ill. He became weaker and weaker, as he stayed inside to study. The yearning in his heart grew and grew. At times he was not sure for what he yearned, but it lifted him away from studying the books. The more he disciplined himself to study, the weaker he became. Among the young scholars with whom he studied were two who secretly went among the Hassids. When they saw the rabbi's son so pale and losing heart from learning they asked him what was wrong.

Friends: What is making you so ill?

Rabbi's son: Deep inside I feel a longing that will not go away.

Friends: There is only one man that can help – a holy man who lives one day's journey away. You must go to him for he has the power to release your soul to its destiny.

Rabbi's son: Is he pure?

Friends: We do not know whether he is pure, but we do know that no one leaves him without being helped.

Narrator: The son went to his father, seeking permission to take the trip to the holy man.

Rabbi: What help can he be to you? He is a simple man, not half as learned as you are.

Narrator: The boy returned to his learning, but before long he again felt the deep yearning for something more in his soul. He begged his father to let him go. His father saw that his son was becoming weaker and weaker. It was as if all life was being

	drained out of him. In the end he relented and said that he could visit the holy man.
Rabbi:	However, I will accompany you to protect you. It may be the evil one who is drawing you on this way.
Narrator:	When the cart was laid and the horses had been tied, the rabbi turned to his son:
Rabbi:	If anything happens on our journey we will take it as a sign from God not to continue. If nothing happens it will be a sign that it is a true pilgrimage.
Narrator:	So they started on their journey. However, they hadn't travelled far when one of the horses slipped as they crossed a shallow brook. Rabbi and son were thrown from the cart into the water.
Rabbi:	You see, my son, heaven has sent us a sign. We must return, for this is an evil journey.
Narrator:	The rabbi's son became downcast as he returned home to his studies. Within weeks he became so weak that it was clear he was dying. He went to his father to beg him to try again. His father agreed and they rode on their way. But two-thirds into the journey the wheel got caught in a ditch and the axle of the cart broke.
Rabbi:	This holy man must surely be an imposter for we have another sign from heaven.
Narrator:	They mended the wagon and returned home, where the boy got sicker and sicker. Finally, at death's door, he begged his father to try once more.

Rabbi's son: This time let us agree not to take anything which happens to us as an omen from heaven.

Narrator: The father agreed. They set out on their third journey. The day went well and by nightfall they reached the village near where the holy man lived. They booked into an inn for the night, to eat and rest before journeying to the holy man the next morning. At dinner the rabbi got talking to a merchant.

Rabbi: I have heard that many people come to talk to a wonder-worker who lives near here. Do you know him?

Merchant: Don't mention him. I have just returned from his house. He is an imposter and from the evil one – he even works on the Sabbath.

Narrator: On hearing this the rabbi set his heart against the holy man and started his journey back home. However, his son's heart became so heavy that there was no life left. Within two weeks of arriving home the boy died. One night, as the grieving rabbi slept, his son appeared to him in a dream. He was angry.

Rabbi: Son, why are you so angry?

Rabbi's son: Go to that holy man to whom I longed to go.

Narrator: When the rabbi woke he thought to himself that it was probably a chance dream and he did not go. The next night he had the same dream. When he awoke he convinced himself that it was from the evil one. When again on the third night his son appeared to him, the rabbi knew that he must go. As he neared the village he met the merchant

Values for society

	whom he had met at the inn. He spoke in mocking laughter.
Merchant:	Ah, the rabbi is here again, and this time he is alone.
Rabbi:	Are you not the merchant whom I met here once before?
Merchant:	Indeed I am. If you like I will swallow you.
Rabbi:	Who are you?
Merchant:	Do you remember how you and your son once rode to see the holy man, and your horse tripped and fell in the brook? And yet your son made you go on a second journey and on that journey your cart's axle broke. And the third time you met me here and I told you that the man was not holy. Then you turned back once more, and so your son died of a broken heart and loneliness. Go rabbi, now that I have got rid of your son you may journey on to the wonder worker.
Narrator:	With these words the stranger vanished. The rabbi continued on his journey to the holy man.

Reflections

- Instead of creating barriers between people like the old rabbi did, celebrate differences and learn from each other.

- Differences work together. Culture enriches our lives. Just imagine how boring, dull and grey this world would be if we were all the same.

Values for society

- *We have to face the fact that all of us are going to die together or we are going to learn to live together and if we are to live together we have to talk.*
  (Eleanor Roosevelt, 1884–1962, American humanitarian and wife of the US President)

- *After all, there is but one race – humanity.*
  (George Moore)

61. Love thy neighbour

Theme: Resolving conflicts

Introduction

Throughout life we all have to deal with conflicts. They may be between people we work with. Sometimes there may be conflicts within our own families. How are we going to deal with them?

This reading explores the difference between two attitudes of mind – the desire to seek revenge and the command to love your enemies.

Reading

You may hear someone say, 'It's a tough world we live in. You have to stick up for yourself, because if you don't people will take advantage of you.' Have you ever heard the saying, 'An eye for an eye, and a tooth for a tooth'? It comes from the Jewish Bible (Exodus 21). It is taken as a 'tit for tat' rule – a justification to seek revenge on those who harm you. However, the saying has been misunderstood. 'An eye for an eye, and a tooth for a tooth' was not an excuse to seek revenge, but a law that prevented a victim seeking more vengeance than was reasonable. It was a warning that when people sought justice they shouldn't ask for more than they were entitled to.

How would you feel if you were asked to forgive your enemy? In the Christian Bible, Jesus recommended another form of justice. 'You have heard that it was said, "Love your friends, hate your enemies." But now I tell you: love your enemies and pray for those who persecute you, so that you may become the sons of your Father in heaven. You must be perfect – just as your Father in heaven is perfect.' (Matthew 5:43–48)

Jesus regarded vindictiveness – the desire to seek revenge – as a poison. Revenge is not sweet but, instead, causes further harm.

Ill will creates more ill will. There is never a way out of the vicious cycle. Jesus taught a different law: love your enemies as well as your friends. He taught that vengeance belonged to God alone. Jesus's teaching is radical, it is revolutionary.

Reflections

- *An eye for an eye and we'll all be blind.*
  (Mohandas K. Gandhi, 1869–1948, Indian spiritual and political leader)

- *Means are not to be distinguished from ends. If violent means are used, there will be bad results.*
  (Mohandas K. Gandhi, 1869–1948, Indian spiritual and political leader)

- Is Jesus's teaching realistic in today's world?

- *The most revolutionary statement in history is 'Love thine enemy.'*
  (Eldridge Cleaver, b.1935, American civil rights activist)

Part 4

Rights and responsibilities

62. Human rights

Theme: Concern for human rights

Introduction

Human rights are basic rights which many societies believe that people should have. On 10 December 1948 the United Nations General Assembly proclaimed the first ever Universal Declaration of Human Rights. It was written as a result of the Second World War that had seen many human rights abused and disowned. So what effect has the Universal Declaration had since 1948 in improving the respect of nations and individuals for human rights?

This reading examines what moves have been made since 1948 to protect people's human rights and suggests areas where improvement is still necessary.

Reading

Consider what has happened since the writing of the Declaration:

- In 1948 Chile was the scene of anti-democratic protests led by the regime of General Pinochet. At the time of writing Pinochet is under arrest in the UK.

- In 1948 Lebanon was a cauldron of war, killing, assassination and disruption of democracy. Now Lebanon is peaceful and is run as a democracy.

- Pakistan has abolished corporal punishment and the use of fetters in prison.

- The apartheid regime has come to an end in South Africa and was removed by peaceful means.

Rights and responsibilities

In many countries of the world more and more articles of the Declaration are being put into practice. Countries are being held to account for their actions. The United Nations continues to ask difficult questions of countries about their religious intolerance, racism, sale of children, child prostitution, violence against women and freedom of expression. Some countries may continue to do horrible and brutal things but they know that someone is watching, whereas 50 years ago no one paid attention. Human rights have taken a giant leap forward in many parts of the world.

However, a lot still remains to be done. Consider the following facts.

- Newspaper and television news bulletins provide daily evidence of how human rights are being abused somewhere in the world.

- In many countries there is no free press.

- Many countries do not hold free elections.

- Unemployment is rife in many parts of the world.

- Large numbers of people in employment are poorly paid.

- Millions of people have barely enough food to live on.

- Too many children are denied education.

- Today people are still persecuted for religious, racial and political reasons.

- Slavery still exists in many countries.

- Torture is carried out in prisons in too many countries.

- Many people are denied their legal rights.

- Freedom of movement between and within countries is denied or restricted for millions.

- Private property is seized and confiscated.

- Genocide continues to destroy whole countries as we have witnessed in Bosnia.

Each one of these is a breaking of one of the articles of the Universal Declaration of Human Rights.

Reflection

- *Imagine you are in charge of a community and are given the following twelve 'rights'. Prioritize these rights in order of importance. Which is the most important? Why?*

Right to education
Right to life and personal safety
Right to social welfare
Right to food and water
Right to protection from torture and inhuman treatment
Right to freedom of expression, conscience and religion
Right to protection of women's human rights
Right to freedom of movement
Right to work
Right to healthcare and services
Right to protection from arbitrary arrest and detention

63. Be or do? That is the question

Theme: Taking personal responsibility for who you will be each day

Introduction

When you got up this morning what were the first things you thought about? Try to remember your first thoughts. Did you think about how you should act today or what you were going to do?

This reading explores the differences between 'being' and 'doing'. It suggests that modern society puts a lot of importance on doing things, at the expense of encouraging people to think about the sort of person they are becoming.

Reading

Consider the following statements.

- In the last fifteen years the average working week has increased by over ten hours to nearly 50 hours.

- Six out of ten men and four out of ten women work on Saturdays.

- Sunday is no longer a day of rest – many people work on Sundays.

- Once upon a time we worked to live. Now we live to work.

- Sundays are boring – there's nothing to do.

- To rest we go to the gym for a 'work out'.

Today people spend more and more time 'doing' rather than 'being'. Success is often associated with achievement, giving the impression that if you have not achieved you have not succeeded.

This trend to emphasize 'doing' above 'being' can also be seen in little everyday things. For example, how many of you made decisions about what clothes to wear or whether to have a shower in your wake-up list? These are 'doing' things. How many of you put down what you wanted to 'be' today? In other words, what sort of day did you decide to have today?

What is the relationship between the time you spend preparing your body for the day – washing, feeding, dressing – and the time you spend preparing your heart and mind for the day – your attitudes and thoughts?

Reflection

- You can decide what sort of day you are going to have and what type of person you are going to be today. Take some time to make up your mind what sort of a day you are going to have. Decision is power. Be!

64. The golden rule

Theme: Responsibility of each person to love their neighbour

Introduction

Each of the major world religions contains a golden rule – a basic rule about how people should treat each other. The following versions come from Judaism and Christianity.

Reading

Once upon a time a non-Jewish man approached the great Rabbi Shammai and said, 'You can convert me to Judaism so long as you teach me the whole truth while I am standing on one foot.' Rabbi Shammai became angry at the insult – that the man thought he could learn all the riches of the Jewish faith whilst standing on one foot. He threw him out.

The man then went to Shammai's rival, Rabbi Hillel, and asked him the same question, 'Convert me to Judaism whilst I stand on one foot.' Rabbi Hillel replied, 'What is hateful to you, do not do to your neighbour.'

Years earlier another teacher answered the question in a very similar way. A religious scholar approached Jesus and asked, 'What must I do to get to heaven?' Jesus asked the man, 'What does it say in your holy text?' The scholar replied, 'That you love your God with all your heart, mind and soul, and that you love your neighbour as well as you do yourself.' 'Good answer!' said Jesus. 'Do it and you'll live.' This has become a central teaching within Christianity.

The scholar went on to try to trap Jesus. 'Who is my neighbour and what does it mean to show love?' Jesus replied by telling a story. 'There was once a man travelling from Jerusalem to

Rights and responsibilities

Jericho. The journey took him through a dangerous valley in which bandits and robbers used to hide. On his way he was attacked by robbers who took his clothes, beat him up and left him for dead. Fortunately a priest came along the way, but when he saw the injured man he crossed to the other side and passed by. Next came a religious teacher. He also avoided the injured man.

'Finally a Samaritan came along the road. When he saw the man his heart went out to him. He gave him first aid and bandaged his wounds. Then he put him on his donkey and took him to an inn. There he paid for his stay and told the innkeeper to take good care of him.'

And Jesus asked the religious scholar, 'What do you think? Which of the three acted as the neighbour to the injured man?' 'The one whose heart went out to him, bandaged his wounds and took him to the inn.' Jesus said, 'Go and do the same.'

Reflections

- In order to act responsibly towards each other we need to deepen our concern for the welfare of others. It is not a matter of thinking clearly. It is a matter of feeling correctly. For example, you know that the Nazis killed millions of people in the Second World War. There was something seriously wrong in the way the Nazis felt towards others.

- *No man is a true believer unless he desireth for his brother that which he desireth for himself.*

(Muhammad, 570–632, Prophet of Islam)

65. A depressing trend

Theme: Responsibility towards each other

Introduction

'I felt as if no one could ever like me. Everything felt so dark. I started to wonder what the point of it all was.'

A thirteen-year-old girl wrote these words. In one sense she was fortunate. Her depression was recognized and she was given help. However, many more young people who feel hopeless and isolated do not get the help they need. Sometimes feelings of depression drive children to take their own lives.

The following reading explores what it feels like to be depressed, through the eyes of one teenager. It shows how easy it is for each of us to hurt each other and demonstrates the need for people to take care of each other.

Reading

Cora's story

I feel that I have to do very well in my studies for my dad because if I fail I feel like I let him down and that's the worst feeling I ever felt. My fear of failure is also about getting my homework done or not. My parents have so many expectations of me, to do well in school, to get into a good college. It makes it even harder to enjoy school.

What makes me angry and sad is that I don't have a real friend. I hang around with different people and talk, but I don't have anyone I can really express my feelings to. If I tell anybody a secret they'll blurt it out or tell their other friends. It makes me cry sometimes. People think I'm friends with Rosie and Ann but I'm not. They dumped me like a sack of potatoes when they pretended to be my friends. Rosie talks to me like I'm stupid and talks behind my back to Ann.

Rights and responsibilities

Sometimes I compare myself with other people and get depressed that I'm not as pretty as them or don't have nice clothes like they do.

Reflections

- How can you tell if someone is depressed? What signs would you look out for?

- What pressures do you think exist today, which make some teenagers depressed? Consider whether any of the following can lead a person into feeling bad about themselves and maybe feeling depressed:

    being bullied
    problems with school and exams
    anxiety about what the future holds
    family problems, and a lack of time which parents spend with their children discussing day-to-day life.

- Do you ever feel like Cora? In groups, discuss what advice you could give to her. What are some healthy ways to deal with stress and feelings of depression?

- Teen depression was once virtually unknown, or, at least, went unrecognized. It is now becoming a feature of modern life. Many young people become depressed because they don't have adequate ways to deal with life's small defeats and setbacks – a bad mark, an argument with parents, being rejected by a friend. We each need to learn how to handle our relationships with others skilfully.

- We all feel down and sad at times. What is important is that we learn to take care of each other, and take responsibility for being good friends together.

66. The chest of broken glass

Theme: Responsibilities between children and parents

Introduction

The responsibilities between parents and their children change throughout life. Parents have responsibilities to care for their children and to bring them up in a secure environment. However, responsibility is a mutual relationship. Children also have responsibilities towards their parents, as the following story illustrates.

Reading

There was once an old man whose wife had died years earlier. He lived on his own. Most of his friends were already dead. Although he had worked hard throughout his life he had been hit by misfortune. Now he was old he could no longer work to support himself. He had three sons but he rarely saw them. They had grown up and left home to have their own families. They all lived in other towns and had become so involved in their own lives that they had little time for their father.

Gradually the old man grew weaker and weaker, and his sons came to visit him less and less. It was clear that they didn't want to be around him because they were frightened that he would become a burden. He stayed up all night worrying what would become of him. Then he hit upon a plan.

The next morning he went to see his friend the carpenter and asked him to make a large chest. Then he went to his friend the glass blower and asked him for all his broken pieces of glass. Finally he went to the locksmith and asked for an old lock. He took the chest home and put it under the window. He filled it with the glass and locked it tight.

Rights and responsibilities

The next time his sons came to dinner they inquired about the chest. 'What's in the chest?' 'Oh, nothing. Just some things I have been saving.' The sons talked amongst themselves. They knew that their father lived a very simple life. Where had all his earnings gone to? All that they could think was that he had stored his wealth in the chest. 'It must be full of gold that he has been saving for years.'

The sons talked it over and realized that they must protect their inheritance. And so each son in turn went to live with his father to look after him. They cooked him the best meals and tended to his every need. In time their father grew very sick and died. The sons gave him a very nice funeral. After all, they had a fortune sitting under the window, they could afford to splash out.

After the funeral the three sons gathered around the chest. The eldest took a pair of pliers and broke the lock. And, of course, they found it full of broken glass. The eldest son was very angry. 'What a mean trick. What a cruel thing to do to your own sons!' The middle son defended his father. 'What else could he have done? We had abandoned him. If it wasn't for the chest we would have neglected him until his death.' 'I'm so ashamed of myself,' sobbed the youngest son. 'We forced him to lie to us in order to get us to care for him.'

The eldest son emptied the chest to make sure there was no hidden treasure. When all the glass was spilt out on the floor the three brothers silently stared at the inscription on the bottom of the chest: 'Honour thy mother and father.'

Reflections

- What do you think it means to 'honour thy mother and father'?

- In the past, old people were looked after in the family home. Today it is common for the elderly to spend their last years in old people's homes or nursing homes. What does this say about modern society?

67. The old grandfather and his grandson

Theme: Respect for others

Introduction

What do you think makes a good person?

Some people may say that they have a good heart, as opposed to people who have hearts of stone. Each of the major religions contains a version of the golden rule: 'Do unto others as you would have them do to you.' A good person is therefore someone who thinks of others. A person with a good heart demonstrates skills of empathy, an ability to put themselves into the shoes of others, to experience life as they see it. A good person is a person who desires goodness – who lives up to the golden rule, and has respect for others.

The famous Russian novelist, Leo Tolstoy, told a story about an old grandfather and his grandson, which captures this quality.

Reading

The grandfather had become very old. His legs wouldn't go, his eyes didn't see, his ears didn't hear, he had no teeth. And when he ate, the food dripped from his mouth.

The son and daughter-in-law stopped setting a place for him at the table and gave him supper in the kitchen. Once they brought dinner down to him in a cup. The old man wanted to move the cup and dropped and broke it. The daughter-in-law began to grumble at the old man for spoiling everything in the house and breaking the cups and said that she would now give him dinner in a dishpan. The old man only sighed and said nothing.

One day the husband and wife watched as their small son started playing on the floor with some wooden planks: he was building something. The father asked, 'What is that you are doing, Misha?' And Misha said, 'Dear Father, I am making a dishpan. So that when you and dear Mother become old, you may be fed from this dishpan.'

The husband and wife looked at one another and began to weep. They became ashamed of so offending the old man, and from then on seated him at the table and waited on him.

Reflections

- What does this story have to say to us?

- Try to think of times in your life when you have failed to respond to somebody because you have been so preoccupied with your own interests.

- If respect for others is one of the values that characterizes a good person, what characterizes a not-so-good person?

68. King Richard and the horseshoe nail

Theme: Taking responsibility for one's actions

Introduction

Today people often talk about their 'rights'. What we don't hear much about is people's responsibilities. A person's responsibilities extend to their actions and their relationships.

Responsibility is the willingness to accept the results of your actions. It means accepting a task and doing it to the best of your ability. To act responsibly towards people means to take your commitments towards them seriously. Responsible people don't make excuses when things go wrong.

People develop responsibility as they develop any other values – through practice. The following story illustrates what happens when people do not take responsibility – even for the small things in life.

Reading

Narrator: King Richard III of England was about to go into battle against Henry, the Earl of Richmond. He sent his groom to get his favourite horse saddled. When the groom arrived at the stables he was told that the horse was not ready. So many horses had been used over the past few days that there was no more iron left to make horseshoes.

Groom: The King's enemies are fast approaching. Make do with what iron you have.

Narrator: So the blacksmith forged together all the scraps of iron in his workshop. There was just enough to make four horseshoes. However, as he counted the nails to knock into the shoes he discovered that he was one or two nails short.

Rights and responsibilities

Groom: I have already told you that we do not have time to wait. The King's enemies are nearly at the city gates. Make do with what you have.

Blacksmith: I can put them on, sir, but the fourth shoe will not be very secure.

Groom: Just nail it on, and hurry, or the King will be angry with both of us.

Narrator: And so the blacksmith did as he was told, securing the fourth horseshoe as best he could. King Richard led his men into the thick of battle. Many men were slain on either side of him. As he turned his horse to go up the hill the fourth horseshoe came loose and the horse stumbled and fell. Richard was thrown to the ground. Before he could grab the reins the frightened horse had run off. He waved his sword in the air.

Richard: A horse! A horse! My kingdom for a horse!

Narrator: Within seconds Henry's soldiers were upon Richard and the battle was over.

And since that time, people have said,

For want of a nail, a shoe was lost,
For want of a shoe, a horse was lost,
For want of a horse, a battle was lost,
For want of a battle, a kingdom was lost,
And all for the want of a horseshoe nail.

Reflection

- Be responsible for all of your actions. Do not overlook the small duties. Many a person has met their downfall through failing to pay attention to the little things.

69. The human organ scandal

Theme: Rights over your own body

Introduction

Do you have the right to do what you like with your own body? Listen to the following story and consider your own reactions. It is about whether a person has the right to donate their own organs after death to whoever they wish.

Reading

To give someone the gift of life by donating your own organs is the last act of generosity which many people feel they can perform. However, relatively few people donate their organs. It is a matter of choice. Many people do not think of it. Of those who do, few take the trouble to make the necessary arrangements. Some people find it difficult to think about their relatives being cut up after their death. Others believe that their body is their own, to do with as they wish. In 1999 there were 6700 people in Britain on waiting lists for organ transplants. The previous year there had been only 847 organs donated. There is, therefore, a great shortage of organs, and many people die whilst waiting for a transplant.

In the summer of 1999 a scandal erupted over the donation of human organs. One donor, a white man, insisted, through his family, that his organs should be given only to a white person. It is believed that three patients received the donor's heart, liver and kidneys in separate operations. The donor was roundly condemned as being racist. But didn't he have the right to do what he wished with his own body parts?

Both the Health Secretary and the British Medical Association reacted sharply to the incident. The Health Secretary said that, if necessary, he would introduce new laws to keep racism out of blood transfusions and organ donations.

There is another side to the story. Since it is a matter of choice, doesn't a person have a right to stipulate that they want their kidneys to be given to a person of a particular colour – be it white, black, brown or yellow? Doesn't a person have a right to lay down certain conditions about who receives their organs? After all, many people practise similar freedoms of choice in their everyday life: for example, who they sell their car or house to, which shops they decide to buy from. We practise freedom of choice when we choose the charity to which we donate money. Shouldn't we have the same freedom to choose the kind of person to whom we will donate our body parts? The argument has to be balanced carefully with the dangers to which freedom of choice may give rise. There is a very real danger that one person's right to freedom of choice could be used to damage and abuse others.

Reflections

- Do you think this incident was racist? Should the hospital have refused to accept the organs? Does the donor have a right to set down conditions for the use of his or her organs?

- With so few organs available, many doctors feel that donating such organs as your kidneys should not be a matter of choice, but compulsory. What do you think? Do you think it is a good idea that people should be made to help others by donating their organs once they are dead?

70. It's my heart

Theme: Rights over one's own body

Introduction

You might say, 'It's my body I can do what I want with it!' But can you? Anyone who is eighteen or over has the right to refuse medical treatment so long as they are mentally 'competent'. However, the law is more complicated for people under eighteen.

Children are allowed to give consent for medical treatment, without their parents' knowledge, if they are thought to be mature enough. This means that a fifteen-year-old could give consent for a blood transfusion even if the parents refused on religious grounds. It is up to the doctors and courts to judge if a child is mature enough. Although children have the right to give consent they do not have the right to refuse medical treatment.

In the following reading a fifteen-year-old girl was made to have a new heart against her own wishes. The story raises the question, 'Whose body is it anyway?'

Reading

A fifteen-year-old girl was forced to have a heart transplant after she contracted an infection which damaged her heart beyond repair. It all happened in such a short space of time. In a matter of weeks the girl had changed from being a healthy teenager who loved netball and swimming to become a very sick patient with only weeks to live. Her only hope was a heart transplant. However, the girl refused. In a statement she made to lawyers by her bed she said:

I understand what a heart transplant means ... check-ups ... tablets for the rest of your life. I feel depressed about that. I am only fifteen and I don't want to take tablets for the rest of my life. It's all happened so quickly. If I don't have the operation I will die. I really don't want a transplant. I am not happy with it.

Rights and responsibilities

Death is final – I know I can't change my mind. I don't want to die but I would rather die than have the transplant and have someone else's heart. I would rather die with fifteen years of my own heart. If I had someone else's heart I would be different from anyone else. I would feel different with someone else's heart. That's a good enough reason not to have a heart transplant, even if it saved my life.

(quoted in *Daily Mail*, 16 July 1999)

After the girl's parents had failed to persuade her to have the operation Newcastle City Hospitals NHS Trust took the case to a high court judge who gave the go-ahead for the operation.

Reflections

- Do you think the judge had the right to impose a heart transplant on the girl against her wishes?

- Why do you think that the doctors were so anxious to carry out the operation and not abide by the girl's wishes? Do you think they were right? Do doctors have the right to do what they consider best or should the patient's wishes always be the determining ones?

- The legal age for sexual consent is sixteen, and for homosexuals it is eighteen. There is also talk of giving sixteen-year-olds the right to vote. So why do you think fifteen-year-old children have the right to give consent for medical treatment but not the right to refuse? Is this a sensible legal ruling?

- The girl was amazingly brave. A lot of people fear death so much that they will do anything to run away from it. The fifteen-year-old was willing to face death in the full knowledge of what she was doing. What would you have done in a similar situation? What thoughts would have guided your decision?

- Many religions of the world teach that our bodies are gifts from God. We are not free to do what we like with our bodies. Instead, we should act as responsible stewards.

71. Storm over the 'morning after' pill

Theme: Whose rights should be protected?

Introduction

Britain has become the first country in the world to allow women to keep supplies of the 'morning after' pill in their bathroom cabinets in case of emergencies. The 'morning after' pill is a contraceptive which can be used up to three days after having sexual intercourse. Research suggests that it is most effective if it is used within twelve hours. However, this new freedom raises some crucial moral questions.

This reading considers both sides of the argument.

Reading

The 'morning after' pill has to be prescribed by a doctor and, until this new initiative became law, these pills were only available to women who attended clinics up to three days after having unprotected sex. This new move makes the pill available for the cost of a £10 payment. The course of four pills, taken over twelve hours, is the equivalent of a week's worth of the contraceptive pill and can be obtained from any of the British Pregnancy Advisory Service clinics. The pills prevent pregnancy by stopping the egg implanting in the womb.

The initiative to provide 'morning after' pills was originally aimed at helping busy career women, so that they can be prepared for the unexpected. However, concerns have been raised by campaigners for family and pro-Life groups, that it would be used by teenaged girls and that the move by the British Pregnancy Advisory Service was 'reckless' and that it would encourage young girls to have casual sex. Pro-Life groups have spoken against the scheme, saying that it shows a disregard for the rights to life of the unborn child. Others are concerned that the scheme will put more people at risk from sexually transmitted diseases.

Promoters of the pill stress that it is not a method of abortion. They point to the fact that in 1998 189,000 pregnancies ended in abortion, and that making the pill more widely available would cut the number of unwanted pregnancies, especially among teenage girls. However, others have seen the introduction of the pill as an excuse for people to plan to be irresponsible.

Reflections

• What message does the availability of the 'morning after' pill give people? Do you think it is helping people to act irresponsibly?

• Do you think there is a danger that people will start abusing this pill and become more careless?

• Whose 'rights' are being protected by this new move?

72. Condoms for homosexual prisoners

Theme: Rules, law and human rights (the rights of a prisoner)

Introduction

Almost everyone agrees that people who have committed crimes should be punished. A variety of reasons are given. Some believe that prison should help the criminal reform, and become a better person. Others believe that criminals need to be put in prison in order to protect society from their crimes. Prison also acts as a form of deterrent, discouraging other possible offenders from committing crimes. By putting a person in prison you are taking away some of their freedoms. The question is, how many freedoms should you take away?

In July 1999 a British judge ruled that homosexual prisoners should be allowed to have condoms provided. The story raises a crucial issue: what rights should prisoners have?

Reading

On Monday 5 July 1999, Mr Justice Latham said that the Prison Service had wrongly refused Glen Fielding, 37, a practising homosexual, condoms.

In the High Court the Judge ruled that homosexual prisoners should be provided with condoms if they were at risk of having unsafe sex. He went on to state that this was not to promote homosexual sex amongst prisoners but to prevent the spread of AIDS and other sexually transmitted diseases. The Judge accepted that according to the European Human Rights Convention a person has a right to express their sexuality in a safe way.

Judge Latham's ruling caused an outcry from morality campaigners who warned that it would lead to increased gay sex between prisoners.

Reflections

- What rights do you think prisoners (a) should lose, (b) should retain inside prison?

- Most heterosexual prisoners who lose their liberty are prevented from expressing their sexuality. However, this is not the case for homosexual prisoners. Do you think Judge Latham was right in his judgement?

73. Date rape

Theme: Do friends have special rights, or is it just a simple matter of abuse?

Introduction

Date rape is the term used when a person goes out with someone on a date, and is raped by them. According to the statistics it is Britain's fastest-growing reported crime. According to Home Office figures nearly four in ten rape victims were raped by someone they knew.

The following reading explores some of the issues around date rape and asks whether people have a right to expect sex from a person they are going out with or whether such expectations are just another form of abuse.

Reading

Only six in every hundred reported rapes lead to a conviction. This has led to a call to reduce sentences where the defendant is known to the victim, in order that there will be more convictions. The government is considering the introduction of a separate offence for date rape cases.

So why is date rape on the increase? Some point to the casual way that people treat sex. Teenagers are being bombarded with sexual messages. Explicit teenage magazines, television soap operas and films create an atmosphere of sexual promiscuity. In today's society it is seen as the norm for a man and woman to meet at a nightclub, dance provocatively and then end up in one of their homes.

A survey of young men revealed that many thought it was acceptable physically to force a woman into sex if they know her. One in eight men could imagine themselves forcing their girlfriends to have sex, and one in six could imagine themselves forcing their wives to have sex. Both are, however, illegal.

Furthermore, one in ten men could imagine themselves forcing a woman to have sex if they knew they weren't going to be found out. Some men revealed that they thought they had a right to have sex if they had spent a lot of money on their 'date'.

So what would happen if the government did create a new law making date rape a specific offence separate from other forms of rape? It would send out a powerful message, that society is not willing to accept such behaviour. There is such a thing as overstepping the boundaries.

Reflections

• Do you think that anyone has a 'right' to have sex? What if their partner doesn't want to? Does a husband or wife have the right to force their partner to have sex?

• Why do you think some people regard rape as one of the worst crimes one person can inflict on another? Do you think date rape counts as domestic violence and abuse?

74. Whose life is it anyway?

Theme: The right to die or end one's own life

Introduction

Euthanasia is the practice of bringing on a gentle and easy death, especially when a person is incurably ill and in a lot of pain. The person can die with dignity, at a time of their own choosing. The word comes from two Greek words: eu meaning good and thanatos meaning death. Euthanasia is therefore a 'good death' – a choice made by the patient to end their life well rather than endure suffering. In the UK euthanasia is illegal. Although there is a range of views on the subject amongst doctors, the majority of opinion in the profession remains strongly against it.

Late in November 1998 American TV viewers watched Thomas Youk, a terminally ill cancer patient, receive a fatal injection from Dr Jack Kevorkian, known as 'Dr Death' for his role in 130 assisted suicides. After Mr Youk's death he challenged the legal system, saying, 'I want to be prosecuted for euthanasia. I am going to prove that this is not a crime, ever.' (Daily Telegraph, 14 April 1999). In April 1999 'Dr Death' was sentenced to 10 to 25 years in prison.

Cases like 'Dr Death' have re-opened the euthanasia debate . However, not all cases are as dramatic, as this reading illustrates.

Reading

One Sunday during October 1998, Victoria Wood, 56, brought her husband Tim, 67, back to their house from the nursing home. He was suffering from a severe form of Parkinson's disease. She cooked him tea, put on his favourite music and then took him to bed. She gave him some sleeping pills and then they got undressed and lay by each other. Then Victoria told Tim how much she loved him and put a pillow over his face, trying to smother him. But Tim struggled. He woke, gasping, finding it difficult to breathe and then fell off the bed.

Victoria was concerned that Tim had hurt himself and so she called an ambulance. When it arrived she told the paramedics that she had tried to kill her husband, adding that she had failed him. It was this confession which led her to the courtroom, and a sentencing of two years' probation for attempted murder. As a result Vicki will probably never see her husband alone again. She has to be chaperoned on all of her visits to the nursing home.

In the early stages of Tim's illness the couple had talked about euthanasia. They joined the Voluntary Euthanasia Society, and both signed 'living wills' – a document in which you declare what you want to happen to your body under certain medical circumstances. Tim was clear in his own mind that he never wanted to go into a home, nor be treated with any drugs other than painkillers. He wanted his life to end when there was still some quality left. Vicki remembers the time when she asked Tim to write down the point after which he would not wish to go on. He wrote that it would be when he could no longer take his dog for a walk and find his way home.

After all that she has been through Vicki still supports euthanasia, in the belief that people should be allowed to make their own personal choice. Whose life is it anyway?

Reflections

- Should terminally ill patients have a right to take their own life? If society treats euthanasia as a crime isn't it denying people a basic right?

- Article 3 of the Universal Declaration of Human Rights declares, 'Everyone has the right to life.' Is this right more important than the right to choose to die?

- Why do you think that the majority of doctors are opposed to euthanasia? Whose rights may they be protecting? What might be the (ethical) dangers of euthanasia?

- If doctors should always act in their patients' best interests, shouldn't they help terminally ill patients to die well, if that is their wish?

75. Ruby Bridges' walk to school

Theme: A commitment to civil rights

Introduction

Sometimes it is easy to feel that we have no influence in the great big scheme of things. It is tempting to feel that we are insignificant. At such times it is important to remember that many of the big changes in society have been brought about by ordinary people trying to do their best.

The following incident took place in America in 1961. It was a time of great social unrest as black people fought for their right to be treated equally with white people. Passions were high.

Reading

Ruby Bridges was only six when she became famous. She was the only black child going to an all-white school. She lived in New Orleans, America, at a time when schools were segregated: there were smart schools for whites, in fashionable areas, from which black people were excluded.

Each morning federal marshals arrived at Ruby's home to take her to school. For days that turned into weeks – and weeks that turned into months – Ruby had to walk up to school and be heckled by mobs of adults. For the best part of a year she attended school all by herself because of a total boycott by white families. And yet Ruby persisted. As she was escorted through the mobs on her way to and from school she remained calm. She didn't react to the vicious jibes demanding that 'dirty niggers' get out of their school.

One day as she walked out of school a woman spat at Ruby but missed. Ruby smiled at her. A man shook his fist at her. Ruby only smiled back. Do you know what she told one of the marshals? She told him that every night before she goes to sleep she prays for those people. When she was asked why she prays for people who are trying to hurt her she replied, 'The minister said God is watching and He won't forget, because He never does. The minister says if I forgive the people, and smile at them and pray for them, God will keep a good eye on everything and He'll be our protection.'

(*The Moral Life of Children*, Robert Cole)

Although Ruby was only six years old at the time she displayed a high degree of moral courage. Like each of us, Ruby had a will and used it to make a moral choice. She demonstrated moral stamina and acted with honour.

Reflections

- What was it in Ruby that gave her the strength to smile when other people in the same situation would have hurled back abuse?

- Ruby used her will to make a moral choice. She showed courage and honour.

- *Never doubt that a small group of thoughtful, committed citizens can change the world. Indeed, it's the only thing that ever has.*

  (Margaret Mead, 1901–1978, American anthropologist)

- *Courage is the strength to face pain, act under pressure, and maintain one's values in the face of opposition. You gain strength, courage and confidence by every experience in which you really stop to look fear in the face. You are able to say to yourself, 'I lived through this horror. I can take the next thing that comes along.'*

  (*You Learn by Living*, Eleanor Roosevelt)

76. A case for civil rights in the UK

Theme: The age of consent – gender equality

Introduction

The legal age of consent for heterosexual sex is sixteen years. However, for homosexuals it is eighteen years. This discrepancy between ages has recently caused a national debate.

Homosexuals believe they are being discriminated against. Article 7 of the Universal Declaration of Human Rights states, 'All are equal before the law and are entitled without any discrimination to equal protection of the law.' The UK is the only country in the European Union to have different ages of consent for homosexual and heterosexual couples.

This reading examines the arguments on both sides of this public debate.

Reading

Before 1967 it was illegal to take part in homosexual acts. However, in 1967 it was made legal for consenting adults aged 21 and above to have homosexual sex. The age was lowered to eighteen in 1994. More recently, a motion went through the House of Commons to lower the age to sixteen, as a result of a ruling in July 1997 by the European Commission on Human Rights that an unequal age of consent was a violation of privacy laws and was discriminatory. But the story does not end there.

On Wednesday 22 July 1998 the House of Lords threw out a move to legalize homosexual sex at sixteen years. Crowds of gay protesters outside the Houses of Parliament greeted the decision with fury. However, Baroness Young, who opposed the idea of lowering the age of consent, said she had been bombarded by letters of support from people of all religious faiths and none. Some homosexuals had also written to back her. She said that it was 'clearly not wanted by the public at large', many of whom were 'quite fearful about what is happening in society'.

Supporters of the motion to lower the age of consent mentioned the following arguments.

(1) It is a matter of treating all people equally. Why should one group of people be allowed to have sex at sixteen and another have to wait until eighteen?

(2) The only reason why people do not want the age of consent to be lowered is because they are 'homophobic' – they have a dislike of homosexuality. Such an attitude is prejudiced and discriminatory and should not be supported by the law.

(3) Making homosexuality illegal encourages secrecy and stops young people from seeking advice and help if they need it.

People who spoke out **against** the lowering of the age of consent mentioned the following arguments.

(1) Making homosexual acts legal at sixteen would make young people vulnerable and put them in danger of being abused by their elders. The law should protect people.

(2) Such a move would undermine the notion of marriage and would encourage young people to take part in society's 'sexual supermarket'.

(3) Such a move would encourage more 'loose living' and would increase the numbers dying of AIDS and other sexual diseases.

Rights and responsibilities

Reflections

- What do you think are the important issues involved here?

- Do you think that sixteen-year-olds are old enough to make the important decision to have sex – be it with a person of the opposite or the same sex?

- Why do you think that some people are 'quite fearful about what is happening in society'?

- Is this a civil rights issue?

77. The sword of Damocles

Theme: The rights and responsibilities of leadership

Introduction

Each of us carries responsibilities throughout life. We all need to be aware of our responsibilities and live up to them. The following story comes from Sicily.

Reading

King Dionysius ruled Syracuse in Sicily. He was wealthy and lived in great grandeur in a beautiful palace, surrounded by great wealth. There were many in his kingdom who were jealous of his good fortune. One of these was Damocles, one of the king's best friends. Dionysius became so fed up with listening to Damocles's jealousy that one day he offered to exchange places with his friend.

'Do you really think I am happier than you?' 'Of course you are,' said Damocles. 'Look at all your great wealth. How can you help but be happy? If I had all your riches I too would be able to live a life without worry.' 'Perhaps you would like to change places with me for one day to see what my life is really like?' 'If I could live like you for even one day I would not want for anything else.'

And so for a day Dionysius and Damocles changed places. The next day Damocles was led to the palace. The servants had been instructed to treat him as the king and to give him anything he wanted – the best food and wine, royal robes and a kingly crown. Damocles wanted for nothing. 'Ah, this is the life. Now I know what it is to be in paradise! I have never enjoyed myself so much.'

Rights and responsibilities

At dinner that evening Damocles was served with the most luxurious food. As he lifted his wine cup to his lips his eyes looked up at the ceiling. There, suspended on a very thin thread, was a sword. Its tip pointed straight towards his forehead. At any moment the thread could break and he would be killed in an instant. All the blood drained from his face. All the luxuries surrounding him meant nothing compared to this threat on his life. He only wanted to run out of the palace as soon as he could.

'What is the matter, my friend?' Dionysius asked. 'That sword, that sword!' exclaimed Damocles. 'Don't you see it?' 'Of course I see it. It hangs there every day and at any time someone or something could snap the thread. It is a constant reminder to me that if I rule unwisely a jealous courtier or adviser could cut the thread. Or someone could spread lies about me and turn the people against me. If you want to be ruler you must be willing to accept these risks. Responsibility and risk are the brothers of receiving power. They go hand in hand.'

'I now realize that leadership involves much more than living in luxury and having an easy life. Please take your place and let me go back home to my own house.' As long as Damocles lived he did not once want to change places with Dionysius again.

Reflections

- What qualities does a good leader have? What qualities would you look for in a king, prime minister or president?

- *To me rule (is) not merely a crown or a mace but an honorable service.*
  (Hussein, 1935–1999, Jordanian king)

- *Anyone who wants to be a leader must be the servant, not the boss, of those he wants to serve.*
  (Aminu Kano, b.1920, Nigerian politician)

78. 'The most sought-after criminal in the world'

Theme: What do you do with a bad world citizen?

Introduction

Not only are we citizens of our own country, we are also global citizens. Sometimes people are found guilty of violating human rights. So what happens when a world citizen does something wrong?

The International Court of Justice, which sits at The Hague in the Netherlands, acts as a world court. It was set up in 1945 under the Charter of the United Nations. Since then the world has been witness to countless atrocities against humanity. This reading describes events in the former Yugoslavia in the 1990s.

Reading

Genocide is the deliberate extermination of a national, ethnical, racial or religious group. The twentieth century witnessed a number of regimes that committed this crime: the Nazis under Hitler, Cambodia, Rwanda, Bosnia and Kosovo.

In May 1999 the International Criminal Tribunal for the former Yugoslavia accused Slobodan Milosevic of being a war criminal. This organization was set up by the United Nations in May 1993 in order to prosecute persons responsible for serious violations of international humanitarian law, on the territory of the former Yugoslavia, since 1991. Tribunal investigators worked for weeks in Macedonia and Albania, collecting evidence from Kosovar refugees of war crimes committed by Serb security forces in Kosovo under the orders of Slobodan Milosevic. He is charged with being responsible for the savage ethnic cleansing in Kosovo.

In June 1999 NATO troops found 60,000 Albanian refugees held by Serbian forces in burnt-out villages that had been turned into

Rights and responsibilities

concentration camps. Serb soldiers were holding them prisoner there so that they could be used as a human shield in the event of a ground war with NATO. The refugees were given ID cards bearing their name and a registration number. The cards stated the name of their prison village.

In June 1999 British soldiers uncovered the site of a massacre of Albanians in the village of Blacrkva. At least 75 men, women and children were believed to have been shot at close range by Serb forces. Albanians fled their homes when Serb forces invaded their village on 25 March 1999. They took refuge in a stream underneath the railway bridge. However, a Serb patrol came across them and opened fire. When Serb troops arrived they separated the men from the women and children and told them to strip. The troops searched their clothes for valuables before shooting them dead.

In July 1999 NATO peacekeepers found a mass grave containing as many as 350 bodies. Serb paramilitaries had swept through the area around Ljubenic killing everything which moved. The 'ethnic cleansing' began on 1 April. For two days the Serb soldiers carried out an orgy of killings.

This was not the first time that political leaders were held responsible for acts carried out by their soldiers. Radovan Karadzic, the Bosnian Serb leader, was accused of genocide, even though he never fired a gun. The charge against Milosevic means that he is regarded as an outlaw in any other country and is liable to be arrested if he travels abroad.

Milosevic and four other Serb leaders have been charged with the deportation of 740,000 Kosovo Albanians and the murder of 340 Kosovo Albanians. United Nations member nations have the responsibility for arresting the five and bringing them to trial in The Hague. If they are found guilty they could be sentenced to jail for life.

Reflections

- What makes an act in war a 'crime'? How should global criminals be treated?

- Does the 'world' have the right to get involved in a particular nation's problems?

- Do you think the idea of a world police force is a good one? What might it achieve? What might its limitations be?

79. Frankenstein foods

Theme: Human responsibility towards the environment

Introduction

Genetically modified (GM) foods are constantly in the news. Headlines warn of 'Frankenstein foods', whilst scientists tell us there is no reason to be alarmed. Each week more and more supermarkets are assuring us that their food is GM-free.

This reading examines the case for and against genetically modified foods.

Reading

For hundreds of years, people have been involved in selective breeding. They have used nature to their own ends. Some would argue that genetically modified foods are exactly this. Take, for example, the average garden tomato. Most tomatoes last only a few days on the supermarket shelf before they start to go off. That is because this is what their genetic make-up causes them to do. Scientists have been able to identify genes in certain varieties of tomato that lengthen the keeping-time of that tomato variety, and transplant it into other types of tomato. This is genetic modification, and is intended to improve the shelf-life of a product.

Genetic modification means that supermarkets won't have to reduce the price of fresh produce so soon after it goes on the shelves, or throw things away so often. The supermarkets will therefore benefit through decreased wastage and thus increased profits. The GM food industry worldwide is big business, worth £30 billion per year.

The numbers of genetically modified foods that are available have been growing for years. Only recently have people started to wake up to this fact and question their trust in such scientific developments. Some people are calling GM food 'Frankenstein food' because it raises the question of whether scientists are playing around with nature, with unknown consequences. Environmental organizations are lobbying to have all GM foodstuffs clearly identified.

Reports recently released suggest that wildlife that feed on GM foods have a shortened life-span. Laboratory tests showed that the life-span of ladybirds that ate greenfly that had fed off GM crops had been reduced by half. Once they were given ordinary greenfly to eat, their life-span went back to normal.

One of the major factors that has enabled farmers in developing countries to grow enough food for increasing populations is that they have used seeds from the previous years' crops. Buying new seeds every year would make it too expensive to feed all the population. GM technology allows seed companies based in the West to produce seeds which can only be used once – they have in-built sterility. This will directly affect farmers in the developing countries.

The genetically modified foods debate is likely to last for a long time.

Reflections

- GM produced foods may have a big impact on the countryside. The prospect of crops that are bug-free will also mean a reduction in the numbers of bigger insects and birds that prey on the bugs. The production of GM foods threatens to destabilize the delicate balance in nature further.

- Are people being responsible in developing GM foods? How might they endanger the environment?

Rights and responsibilities

- Do people have a right to 'tamper with nature'? Instead of redesigning nature for their own convenience, shouldn't humanity be seeking how to work with the grain of nature by making a more sustainable environment?

- There are many advantages in creating GM foods. If you were a scientist what case would you make for GM foods?

- Organizations such as Christian Aid have argued that, instead of helping poor countries, GM crops will actually cause more damage by destroying the rich diversity in nature and the sustainable agricultural systems. What are our responsibilities to these developing countries? Is the GM debate another incidence of the rich West exploiting the developing world?

- This planet is home to all of us – insects, animals and humans. We must learn to share it responsibly with other species.

Part 5
Big questions

80. HAPPINESSISNOWHERE

Theme: Happiness is to be found in the present moment

Introduction

In preparation, write 'HAPPINESSISNOWHERE' on a flipchart or whiteboard and open the assembly by asking pupils to call out what they can see.

Reading

How many of you saw the words 'HAPPINESS IS NOWHERE'?

How many of you saw the words 'HAPPINESS IS NOW HERE'?

The difference between 'happiness is nowhere' and 'happiness is now here' is in your perception, how you see things.

Consider the following thought: 'The gift of happiness is not somewhere out there, it is wrapped up in your heart.' As you look around you, notice those people who find happiness nowhere – they always see the negative side of life – and those who find happiness in the present moment.

Does this mean that some people are born with a happy disposition and others are not? Have you ever noticed how babies enjoy now? In one sense a baby's favourite toy is not a thing but a moment. They have no awareness of the past or the future. Instead *now* is the whole world for the baby, it's their playground. Why wait for heaven when you can have it now?

Can you remember when you were younger, how you marvelled at every new smell, sight and sound? You were full of wonder and imagination, even to the extent of annoying everyone around you with continual questions – 'But why, ... why, ...

Big questions

why ...?' As babies and young children we all had the ability to appreciate what was happening in every present moment: everything was so new to us. When did we lose this sense of wonder?

Reflection

- *The gift of happiness is wrapped in your heart, not the world. Thus, your happiness will never be mailed to you! And it can never get lost in the post! In truth, your happiness has already been delivered, sitting in your inner mail box – your heart – waiting to be opened.*

(*Happiness Now!*, Robert Holden)

81. Nothing can make you happy

Theme: The nature of happiness – where is it to be found?

Introduction

Ask pupils to complete the sentence 'Happiness is … '

We all want to be happy, but do we really know what happiness is and where we are going to find it? This reading asks the question, 'Where is happiness to be found?'

Reading

Look at some of ways we describe happiness:

- 'Really wicked'
- 'I had a hell of a time'
- 'Bad'
- 'It was terribly good'
- 'It was dead good'
- 'Dying to see you'
- 'Unreal'
- 'I nearly died'

What do all these have in common? Do you notice something odd about them?

How we speak reveals how we think. Isn't it odd that we often use the language of pain to describe our happiness. It would appear that we are quite confused about what happiness is. Did you also notice how many of these descriptions identify happiness as though it is 'out there' – being happy is a matter of

Big questions

doing things, seeing people, having experiences. But this is part of the whole confusion about happiness.

Happiness is not something outside you. People and experiences may help you discover your happiness within, but they cannot give you happiness. Notice how easy it is to be lonely, even when you are with a lot of people. Notice how it is possible to be miserable inside even when you are doing things that are fun.

Many people get confused and think that money and possessions can make you happy. But notice how many rich people are also miserable. Money can encourage you to be happy, but it cannot make you happy.

Reflections

• Happiness is not out there. It is here. Happiness is not in things. It is in you. 'No-thing' in the world can make you happy. Everything can encourage you to choose to be happy.

• Choose to be happy now.

82. Life is about …

Theme: The meaning of life

Introduction

Try completing the sentence, 'Life is about … ' Share your ideas with the people around you.

Sometimes it is tempting to equate life's meaning with the number and quality of friends you have, whether you are accepted by people or feel lonely and rejected. Many adults give the impression that the meaning of life involves making money and having a large house. But is life really about these things?

This reading is a piece of advice given to an eighteen-year-old just about to start college.

Reading

Life isn't about keeping score. It's not about how many people call you and it's not about who you've dated, are dating or haven't dated at all. It isn't about who you've kissed, what sport you play, or which guy or girl likes you. It's not about your shoes or your hair or the colour of your skin or where you live or go to school. In fact, it's not about grades, money, clothes or colleges that accept you or not. Life isn't about if you have lots of friends, or if you are alone, and it's not about how accepted or unaccepted you are. Life isn't about that.

But life is about who you love and who you hurt. It's about how you feel about yourself. It's about trust, happiness and compassion. It's about sticking up for your friends and replacing inner hate with love. Life is about avoiding jealousy, overcoming ignorance and building confidence. It's about what you say and what you mean. It's about seeing people for who they are and not what they have. Most of all, it is about choosing to use your

Big questions

*life to touch someone else's in a way that could never have been
achieved otherwise. These choices are what life's about.*

(Jack Canfield in *Chicken Soup for the Teenage Soul*)

Reflections

- Each of us has to take responsibility for who we are. We have
a choice about how we feel about ourselves and towards
others. Each of us should take responsibility for the priorities
we set. We can make a difference to our own lives.

- What do you think 'replacing inner hate with love' means?
How does a person do this?

- *Whenever you do something without asking yourself, 'Why
am I doing this?' – that is meaningless life ... The 'why' of life
makes it meaningful ... Only when an answer is given is one
living life as a man.*

(*The New Life*, Hu Shih)

83. Man's search for meaning

Theme: Making life mean something

Introduction

Viktor Frankl was a great psychiatrist when the Second World War broke out. He was imprisoned for three years in Auschwitz and other concentration camps. Within these camps he saw people who became bitter and angry, who found no meaning in their experience. He also found people who were not only able to survive the horrifying conditions but who found meaning within them. After the war he wrote a book called Man's Search for Meaning. *Here is an extract from it.*

Reading

The experiences of camp life show that man does have a choice of action. We who lived in concentration camps can remember the men who walked through the huts comforting others, giving away their last piece of bread. They may have been few in number, but they offer sufficient proof that everything can be taken from a man but one thing: the last of the human freedoms to choose one's attitude in any given set of circumstances.

If there is a meaning in life at all, then there must be a meaning in suffering. The way in which a man accepts his fate and all the suffering it entails, the way in which he takes up his cross, gives him ample opportunity – even under the most difficult circumstances – to add a deeper meaning to his life. He may remain brave, dignified and unselfish. Or in the bitter fight for self-preservation he may forget his human dignity and become no more than an animal.

What was really needed was a fundamental change in our attitude toward life. We had to learn ourselves and, furthermore, we had to teach the despairing men, that it did not really matter what we expected from life, but rather what life expected from

Big questions

us. We needed to stop asking about the meaning of life, and instead to think of ourselves as those who were being questioned by life – daily and hourly.

(*Man's Search for Meaning: An introduction to logotherapy*, V. Frankl)

Reflections

- How did different people respond to the horrors of the concentration camps? Why did some people lose hope and yet others find a meaning in their existence? What qualities did the two different groups of people have?

- What do you think Frankl means when he says 'What was really needed was a fundamental change in our attitude toward life'? In what ways may his words be useful for people living today?

- *Where I was born, and where and how I lived is unimportant. It is what I have done and where I have been that should be of interest.*

  (Georgia O'Keeffe, 1887–1986, American artist)

84. The child bearer

Theme: Who or what are you going to serve in life?

Introduction

What do you think makes a person great? Is it power, money or fame, or something else?

This reading is about a person whose aim throughout life was to serve the greatest king he could find. During his life he served a number of kings, all with their different demands.

Reading

Narrator: Christopher was born a giant. When he walked he used the trunk of a palm tree as a walking stick, he was that tall! Since he was a young man he had sought to serve the mightiest king on earth. He therefore sought work in the service of the most powerful king around. One day, however, he noticed how the king became frightened when his minstrel sung songs which mentioned the Devil.

Christopher: Who is the Devil and why do you cross yourself every time his name is mentioned? Is the Devil much stronger than you? If so I shall leave you to enter his service.

King: Yes – he is the ruler over all the earth.

Christopher: If he rules over all the earth I must go in search of him for I seek to serve the greatest king. Where do I find him?

King: Oh, don't worry about finding him. If you really want to serve him he will soon find you.

Big questions

Narrator:	Before long the Devil enlisted Christopher into his army. He served his master in all his evil ways – in hatred and deceit, in murder and rape. One day as they travelled along the road they came to a fork in the road. On the right-hand fork Christopher saw a cross with the statue of a man hanging on it. He noticed that the Devil trembled when he saw the cross and hurriedly took the left fork.
Christopher:	Are you afraid?
Devil:	Yes, I fear Christ who is shown on the cross.
Christopher:	If you fear him he must be more powerful than you. I must leave you and serve him.
Narrator:	And so Christopher left the Devil and took the right fork. Soon he saw a beggar and asked him how he could find the Christ figure shown on the cross. The beggar told him to go in search of the hermit at the top of the hill – he knows where you can find Christ. And so Christopher trudged up to the top of the hill. When he reached the hermit he asked:
Christopher:	Is Jesus Christ a great king?
Hermit:	Yes, the greatest – he is the king of the universe.
Christopher:	If that is the case he is the one for whom I have been searching all of my life. Tell me, how do I find him?
Hermit:	Practise fasting and prayer.
Christopher:	This is not my way. I am an action person.
Hermit:	There is one other way, and that is through serving Christ by serving other people.

Christopher: How do I do that?

Hermit: You see that river at the bottom of the hill? Every day people need help crossing the river. You are a big man, serve Christ by helping others cross the river.

Narrator: And so Christopher spent his time helping people across the river. He did this for many years, content to wait until the time when Jesus Christ would come to meet him. One night he was awoken from his sleep in the early hours of the morning by a voice, shouting.

(*Voice:*) Christopher, Christopher, are you there?'

Narrator: Christopher rose from his bed and went outside. He could see no one, and so he went back to bed. Again he heard the voice.

(*Voice:*) Christopher, Christopher, are you there?

Narrator: Again he went outside but saw no one. He returned to bed for the second time. He was disturbed for the third time.

(*Voice:*) Christopher, Christopher, are you there?

Narrator: This time when he went out he saw a small boy on the other side of the river. Faithful to his service he crossed the river to meet the child. He put the boy on his shoulders and started to cross back over. But when he was in the middle of the river the current became stronger and stronger. The boy on his shoulders became heavier and heavier. Christopher staggered under the burden. It took all his strength to carry the boy safely to the other side. When he reached the shore he put the young boy down and asked:

Big questions

Christopher: Who are you? You are so heavy, heavier than if I were carrying the whole world on my shoulders.

Boy: I am the Child Jesus whom you have been seeking and you have indeed carried the sins of the whole world on your shoulders.

Narrator: Christopher had met Jesus whom he had been serving for so many years. He is represented in art carrying the Christ Child on his back. His name, 'Christopher' means 'Christ-bearer'.

Reflections

• As we journey through our lives we have to choose who we are going to serve. Each master – be it money, fame and fortune, food or drink – has his or her own demands.

• We need to decide wisely who we wish to serve in our lives.

85. Truth, Falsehood, Fire and Water

Theme: The struggle between truth and falsehood

Introduction

Each of us experiences the struggle between truth and falsehood. At times we are all tempted to do things that we know are wrong. This tale describes that struggle. It comes from Ethiopia.

Reading

Once upon a time Truth, Falsehood, Fire and Water were travelling along together when they came upon a herd of sheep. They discussed what they should do and decided that the fairest way was to divide the sheep into four groups and each should have one share. And so this is what they did.

No sooner had they divided the herd than Falsehood became greedy and plotted a way of gaining all the sheep for himself. He secretly went to Water and whispered in his ear, 'Fire is planning to destroy all your land and then take your sheep. If I were you I would act quickly and drown him.'

Water foolishly listened to Falsehood and sent a great flood over all of Fire's land. Next Falsehood crept up to Truth. 'Look what Water has done. He has extinguished fire and run off with all his sheep. We should not mix with the likes of Water. Let us take all the sheep and drive them up the mountain.'

Truth foolishly listened to Falsehood and together they drove all the sheep to the top of the mountain. Water tried to run after them, but was trapped since he couldn't run up the mountain. When they got to the top Falsehood turned on Truth and laughed at him. 'You fool, I have tricked you. Now you must hand over all your sheep or else I will destroy you.'

Big questions

In the blink of an eye Truth realized that he had behaved foolishly. 'No! I am not going to give in to you. I will fight you. There is no way I shall be your servant.' And so to this day Truth and Falsehood have fought each other. Sometimes Truth will win. At other times Falsehood will win. But until the end of the world Truth and Falsehood must fight each other, neither resting for fear of the other taking complete control.

Reflections

- Decide today – are you going to speak up for truth or for falsehood?

- *One falsehood spoils a thousand truths.*

(West African proverb)

86. The overflowing cup

Theme: Truth

Introduction

This story records a famous meeting between a Zen Buddhist master and a distinguished professor. It raises the question as to where Truth is to be found.

Reading

Professor: I have travelled far in my attempt to find truth. Can you tell me where I can find it?

Master: Would you like a cup of tea?

Narrator: The Zen Master, with a big smile on his face, started to pour the professor a cup of Indian tea.

Professor: Thank you very much, but I haven't really got time to stay long. I am eager to learn what you have to say to me and then move on. During my whole life I have been searching for truth.

Narrator: The Master continued to pour the tea. The cup was nearly full when the Professor tried to stop him.

Professor: That's enough tea, thank you.

Narrator: But the Master kept pouring.

Professor: Master, the cup is full to overflowing. No more tea will go in.

Narrator: The Master continued to pour until the tea was dripping onto the carpet.

Big questions

Master: Dear Professor, this cup is like your mind. It is so full of your own thoughts and ideas. How can I teach you anything until you empty your cup first?

Reflections

- What did the professor learn from the master about truth that day?

- Are our minds like the professor's, so full that we are not empty enough to learn new ways?

87. What is success?

Theme: Success and fulfillment

Introduction

Ralph Waldo Emerson (1803–1882) was an American poet and a writer of essays. In this poem he speaks about what makes a person successful.

Reading

What is success?
To laugh often and much;
To win the respect of intelligent people
And the affection of children;
To earn the appreciation of honest critics
And endure the betrayal of false friends;
To appreciate beauty;
To find the best in others;
To leave the world a bit better, whether by
A healthy child, a garden patch
Or a redeemed social condition;
To know even one life has breathed
Easier because you have lived;
This is to have succeeded.

Reflection

* *Today I will*
  ... appreciate beauty around me
  ... seek to find the best in others
  ... leave the world a bit of a better place.

88. The Tenth Circle of Hell

Theme: The evil that we can do

Introduction

Look around you at the people with whom you live and work. Do you think it would be possible for you to turn against each other, to start killing each other – people you have lived with and been friends with all of your life?

What happens when societies break down, when people stop working together and start fighting each other?

Well this is exactly what happened in the Bosnian war. This reading is taken from an autobiography of life during this war. Rezak Hukanovic is one of the thousands of Muslim and Croat citizens who witnessed acts of torture in the Serb concentration camps of Omarska and Manjanca in 1992. The Tenth Circle of Hell describes life in the camps. It tells of men made to drink dirty motor oil, of a guard firing into the back of a defenceless man's head and forcing every witness to applaud, and of prisoners being forced to drink their own urine and put their heads through burning tyres.

Reading

It was astonishing to witness the transformation of former friends and acquaintances as they turned into crazed servants of the new (Serbian) authority … Bosnia had long been home to Muslims and Croats as well as Serbs … Until just yesterday Bosnians had shared everything, drinking coffee together, going to parties and funerals together, visiting each other, marrying each other, but now … Bosnia trembled as if it had been hit by a powerful earthquake.

Prisoners were rounded up and moved to Serbian concentration camps. Their only crime was being either Muslim or Croat. The Serbian torturers persecuted the prisoners with multiple acts of humiliation. On one occasion a group of prisoners were made to publicly strip …

Big questions

One big man, over six feet tall , refused to strip. He simply kept quiet and didn't move ... The guard, seeing that the man was steadfast in his intention not to carry out the order ... struck the clothed man in the middle of the head with the rifle butt, once and then again, until the man fell. Then the guard ... moved his hand to his belt. A knife flashed in his hand, a long army knife. He bent down, grabbing hold of the poor guy's hair with his free hand. Another guard joined in ... [They] started using them to tear away the man's clothes. After only a few seconds, they stood up, their own clothes covered with blood. The air resounded with a long, loud, and painful wail. It sent shivers through all who heard it ... The poor man ... tried to stand up, still letting out excruciating screams. He was covered with blood ... the guards had cut off the man's sexual organs and half of his behind ... Later the poor man was taken to a garbage container, doused with gasoline, and burned.

Later in the book she describes torture by Ziga, one of the camp guards.

'On all fours, I said – like dogs!' Ziga bellowed, like a dictator. He forced the three men to crawl up to a puddle ... and then ordered them to wash in the filthy water. Their hands trembling, they washed the blood off their faces. 'The boys have been eating strawberries and got themselves a little red,' said Ziga, laughing like a madman ... Another prisoner, Slavko Ecimovic, a Croat, and one of the first to rebel against local Serb rule, was in the same room where they had just been tortured. At least, it seemed like him. He was kneeling, all curled up, by the radiator. When he lifted his head, where his face should have been was nothing but the bloody, spongy tissue under the skin that had just been ripped off. Instead of eyes, two hollow sockets were filled with black, coagulated blood.

(The Tenth Circle of Hell, R. Hukanovic)

Big questions

Reflections

- The guards were all young men from the surrounding villages. They were Serb volunteers; there were no regular soldiers among them. What makes ordinary people capable of inflicting such torture on people they had previously lived with as friends?

- One prisoner wrote, 'No one, not even God, can pardon them for this.' Do you agree?

- Are all war crimes wrong? Can you think of a situation where breaking the rules of war would be justified? Consider bombing a hospital where a dictator like Hitler is lying ill. Hospitals are granted immunity from attack. But would such a bombing be justified in this case?

89. The end of the world is nigh!

Theme: Prophecies about the future

Introduction

Why have people always wanted to believe that the world is about to end? As the second millennium CE drew to a close, prophets and doomsday cults started to predict the end of the world.

One of the most famous prophets of all time is Nostradamus. His work has recently become very popular. Today's reading explores who Nostradamus was, what he had to say, and what, if anything, he has to teach us today.

Reading

In 1549 a French doctor called Nostradamus began to write a thousand prophecies designed to tell the future history of the world. He lived in the small town of Salon de Provence in the south of France. Today thousands of pilgrims travel to visit his house and to find out about his prophecies. In the last few years, many translations of his prophecies have been published as people try to look into the future and discern their destiny.

What makes Nostradamus stand out from other prophets who have proclaimed the end of the world is his amazing ability for getting things right. Furthermore, he is one of the rare prophets whose forecasts stretched forward through centuries. According to some translations of his prophecies Nostradamus predicted major events throughout history, and many have come true in the twentieth century. Listen to these prophecies.

Nostradamus supposedly prophesied the rise and fall of Hitler:

The greater part of the battlefield will be against Hitler,
He will drag the leader in the cage of iron
When the child of Germany observes no law. (2.24)

Big questions

Some of his prophecies describe specific events and major shifts in political power, such as the Russian Revolution:

And it shall be in the month of October that some great upheaval shall occur.
There shall be extreme change and transformations of kingdoms, and it shall remain so for no more than 73 years and 7 months.

This prophecy does sound like the Russian Revolution that started in October 1917 and lasted 73 years and 7 months, ending in the summer of 1991.

When Iraq invaded Kuwait people found it had already been prophesied by Nostradamus:

Wicked and vile a man of ill repute.
The tyrant of Iraq comes in apace. (8.70)

Where did Nostradamus claim to get his powers of prophecy? We have already mentioned that he trained as a doctor during the time of the plague. It was this plague which killed his wife and two children. These deaths must have had a devastating effect on him and made him question his Christian faith. He searched for answers in both astrology and the occult. At the time when he lived astrology was very popular. Astrologers believed that the place of the stars in the sky could foretell events happening in the world. We also know that Nostradamus used to spend evenings in trances communing with the spirit world. Many believe he got his powers from the spiritual realm.

However, there are others who question whether Nostradamus actually predicted specific events in the future at all. He wrote in sixteenth-century French. Many translations of his prophecies have been made by people who have failed to go back to the first edition of his work or to the original French. Scholars have questioned the accuracy of these translations, pointing out that in many cases people have read into events what they want to see.

Despite this, people today are still eager to read Nostradamus. The Japanese cult leader, Shoko Ashara, who headed the fatal sarin gas attack in the Tokyo subway in April 1995 (killing twelve people and injuring 5500), believed that Nostradamus had foreseen his rise to power. In 1989 he visited France in order to see the original texts for himself. Furthermore, if you visit Hyde Park corner in London you will hear speakers using Nostradamus to proclaim that the end of the world is nigh.

Nostradamus has always attracted people living in times of great uncertainty. There are huge numbers of sites on the Internet about Nostradamus. Such a phenomenon raises certain questions.

Reflections

- Why do you think people have become so concerned about the future?

- Was Nostradamus a prophet? Should people be afraid of what he wrote about the future?

- If there is nothing about this man which is true why would his prophecies have survived so long and had such an impact?

90. Apocalypse now ... or maybe next year!

Theme: Millennium fever

Introduction

At the approach of the year 2000, many people were getting ready for the end of the world. The last three decades of the twentieth century saw the rise of a number of cults proclaiming that the end of the world was very near. The following reading describes some of these cults.

Reading

- In 1993, 76 members of the Branch Davidian cult died in a fire in Waco, Texas. Its leader, David Koresh, believed that God spoke to him personally. Members of the cult believed he was God's chosen one (Messiah).

- In March 1997, in San Diego, California, 39 members of the Heaven's Gate cult committed mass suicide, in the belief that their souls were being transported to a space ship behind the Hale-Bopp comet.

What is going on? Belief that the world is going to end is not new. Christians have always believed that Jesus will come back again and will be accompanied by the apocalypse – dramatic events at the end of time. Saint Matthew's Gospel reports Jesus as saying that his second coming will follow a time of wars, famines, pestilence and earthquakes.

Whilst some people who believe that the apocalypse is very close have strong religious beliefs, many others have no connection with any organized religion. One explanation for people starting to believe that the end is nigh is to do with numbers – a feeling that if some great event is to take place it will happen around the turn of a millennium. The same was the case a thousand years ago.

Polls have shown than one in every ten Americans think it is likely that the world as we know it will end at the millennium, and more than 70 per cent of Christians in America believe that Jesus will return within the next hundred years.

In the last twenty years more and more cults have sprung up heralding events that will bring us closer to the end of the world. More than 1500 new groups have sprung up in the UK in the past 25 years. Some of these are more dangerous than others.

- Police are concerned that the Millennium Dome in Greenwich will become a pilgrimage site for cults and extremists, some bent on committing mass suicide in order to herald in the end of the world.

- The Millennium Watch Institute in Philadelphia, USA, has the names of over 1200 self-styled prophets in its database.

- In October 1998, 78 members of the Concerned Christians cult sold their houses and disappeared from Denver, USA. In January 1999 they resurfaced in Israel. The police accused them of planning an apocalyptic shoot-out in Jerusalem in order to hasten the Second Coming of Christ. In mid-January they were expelled from Israel.

- The Children of God cult now has more than 10,000 members in 40 countries. This cult, which started in 1969, believes that a time of chaos will start in January 2000 that will last until 2007, at the end of which Jesus will return.

Big questions

Reflections

- Public responses to cults have been largely hostile. The media often present them as a threat to society. Why do you think this is the case? In the multi-faith and multi-cultural society in which we live, shouldn't we be more tolerant of religious minorities?

- Do you think it is right that governments are considering introducing legislation to curb cult activities?

- David Koresh's lawyer made the following comment after the events of Waco:

  The true test of a free society is not in how it treats its best citizen but how it treats its worst, its most despised.

  (quoted in *American Studies Today Online*: 'Religious cults in twentieth century America', A.Eyre)

What do you think?

Appendices

Appendix A: **The Universal Declaration of Human Rights**

On 10 December 1948 the United Nations adopted a Universal Declaration of Human Rights. These include the rights to life, liberty and security; freedom from slavery, torture and degrading punishment; the right to equal treatment under the law; the right to education and an adequate standard of living; the right to privacy; freedom of movement, conscience and religion; and the right to take part in government. However, the UN cannot force a country to adopt these rights. What it can do is to make it clear for all the world to see when a country is denying its people any of these rights.

Article 1
All human beings are born free and equal in dignity and rights. They are endowed with reason and conscience and should act towards one another in a spirit of brotherhood.

Article 2
Everyone is entitled to all the rights and freedoms set forth in this Declaration, without distinction of any kind, such as race, colour, sex, language, religion, political or other opinion, national or social origin, property, birth or other status. Furthermore, no distinction shall be made on the basis of the political, jurisdictional or international status of the country or territory to which a person belongs, whether it be independent, trust, non-self governing or under any other limitation of sovereignty.

Article 3
Everyone has the right to life, liberty and security of person.

Article 4
No one shall be held in slavery or servitude; slavery and the slave trade shall be prohibited in all their forms.

Article 5
No one shall be subjected to torture or to cruel, inhuman or degrading treatment or punishment.

Article 6
Everyone has the right to recognition everywhere as a person before the law.

Appendices

Article 7
All are equal before the law and are entitled without any discrimination to equal protection of the law. All are entitled to equal protection against any discrimination in violation of this Declaration and against any incitement to such discrimination.

Article 8
Everyone has the right to an effective remedy by the competent national tribunals for acts violating the fundamental rights granted him by the constitution or by law.

Article 9
No one shall be subjected to arbitrary arrest, detention or exile.

Article 10
Everyone is entitled in full equality to a fair and public hearing by an independent and impartial tribunal, in the determination of his rights and obligations and of any criminal charge against him.

Article 11
Everyone charged with a penal offence has the right to be presumed innocent until proved guilty according to law in a public trial at which he has had all the guarantees necessary for his defence.

No one shall be held guilty of any penal offence on account of any act or omission which did not constitute a penal offence, under national or international law, at the time when it was committed. Nor shall a heavier penalty be imposed than the one that was applicable at the time the penal offence was committed.

Article 12
No one shall be subjected to arbitrary interference with his privacy, family, home or correspondence, nor to attacks upon his honour and reputation. Everyone has the right to the protection of the law against such interference or attacks.

Article 13
Everyone has the right to freedom of movement and residence within the borders of each state.

Everyone has the right to leave any country, including his own, and to return to his country.

Article 14
Everyone has the right to seek and to enjoy in other countries asylum from persecution.

This right may not be invoked in the case of prosecutions genuinely arising from non-political crimes or from acts contrary to the purposes and principles of the United Nations.

Article 15
Everyone has the right to a nationality.

No one shall be arbitrarily deprived of his nationality nor denied the right to change his nationality.

Article 16
Men and women of full age, without any limitation due to race, nationality or religion, have the right to marry and to found a family. They are entitled to equal rights as to marriage, during marriage and at its dissolution.

Marriage shall be entered into only with the free and full consent of the intending spouses.

The family is the natural and fundamental group unit of society and is entitled to protection by society and the State.

Article 17
Everyone has the right to own property alone as well as in association with others.

No one shall be arbitrarily deprived of his property.

Article 18
Everyone has the right to freedom of thought, conscience and religion; this right includes freedom to change his religion or belief, and freedom, either alone or in community with others and in public or private, to manifest his religion or belief in teaching, practice, worship and observance.

Article 19
Everyone has the right to freedom of opinion and expression; this right includes freedom to hold opinions without interference and to seek, receive and impart information and ideas through any media and regardless of frontiers.

Appendices

Article 20
Everyone has the right to freedom of peaceful assembly and association.

No one may be compelled to belong to an association.

Article 21
Everyone has the right to take part in the government of his country, directly or through freely chosen representatives.

Everyone has the right of equal access to public service in his country.

The will of the people shall be the basis of the authority of government: this will shall be expressed in periodic and genuine elections which shall be by universal and equal suffrage and shall be held by secret vote or by equivalent free voting procedures.

Article 22
Everyone, as a member of society, has the right to social security and is entitled to realization, through national effort and international cooperation and in accordance with the organization and resources of each State, of the economic, social and cultural rights indispensable for his dignity and the free development of his personality.

Article 23
Everyone has the right to work, to free choice of employment, to just and favourable conditions of work and to protection against unemployment.

Everyone, without any discrimination, has the right to equal pay for equal work.

Everyone who works has the right to just and favourable remuneration ensuring for himself and his family an existence worthy of human dignity, and supplemented, if necessary, by other means of social protection.

Everyone has the right to form and to join trade unions for the protection of his interests.

Article 24
Everyone has the right to rest and leisure, including reasonable limitation of working hours and periodic holidays with pay.

Article 25
Everyone has the right to a standard of living adequate for the health and well-being of himself and of his family, including food, clothing, housing and medical care and necessary social services, and the right to security in the event of unemployment, sickness, disability, widowhood, old age or other lack of livelihood in circumstances beyond his control.

Motherhood and childhood are entitled to special care and assistance. All children, whether born in or out of wedlock, shall enjoy the same social protection.

Article 26
Everyone has the right to education. Education shall be free, at least in the elementary and fundamental stages. Elementary education shall be made generally available and high education shall be equally accessible to all on the basis of merit.

Education shall be directed to the full development of the human personality and to the strengthening of respect of human rights and fundamental freedoms. It shall promote understanding, tolerance and friendship among all nations, racial or religious groups, and shall further the activities of the United Nations for the maintenance of peace.

Parents have a prior right to choose the kind of education that shall be given to their children.

Article 27
Everyone has the right freely to participate in the cultural life of the community, to enjoy the arts and to share in scientific advancement and its benefits.

Everyone has the right to the protection of the moral and material interests resulting from any scientific, literary or artistic production of which he is the author.

Article 28
Everyone is entitled to a social and international order in which the rights and freedoms set forth in this Declaration can be fully realized.

Article 29
Everyone has duties to the community in which alone the free and full development of his personality is possible.

Appendices

In the exercise of his rights and freedoms, everyone shall be subject only to such limitations as are determined by law solely for the purpose of securing due recognition and respect for the rights and freedoms of others and of meeting the just requirements of morality, public order and the general welfare in a democratic society.

These rights and freedoms may in no case be exercised contrary to the purposes and principles of the United Nations.

Article 30
Nothing in this Declaration may be interpreted as implying for any State, group or person any right to engage in any activity or to perform any act aimed at the destruction of any of the rights and freedoms set forth herein.

Appendix B: UN Convention on the Rights of the Child

On 20 November 1989 the United Nations General Assembly passed the UN Convention on the Rights of the Child. This demands that all actions of a state concerning children should have the best interests of the children at heart. It gives children the civil liberties that adults have in most developed countries. It also demands protection for children from all forms of mistreatment, and requires that children be given an adequate standard of living, good education, health care and also recreation.

Article 1: Definition of Child
Every person under 18, unless national law grants majority at an earlier age.

Article 2: Freedom from Discrimination
Rights in the Convention to apply to all children without exception; the State to protect children from any form of discrimination or punishment based on family's status, activities or beliefs.

Article 3: Best Interests of Child
The best interests of the child to prevail in all legal and administrative decisions; the State to ensure the establishment of institutional standards for the care and protection of children.

Article 4: Implementation of Rights
The State to translate the rights in this Convention into actuality.

Article 5: Respect for Parental Responsibility
The State to respect the rights of parents or guardians to provide direction to the child in the exercise of the rights in this Convention.

Article 6: Survival and Development
The child's right to life; the State to ensure the survival and maximum development of the child.

Article 7: Name and Nationality
The right to a name and to acquire a nationality; the right to know and be cared for by parents.

Appendices

Article 8: Preservation of Identity
The right to preserve or re-establish the child's identity (name, nationality and family ties).

Article 9: Parental Care and Non-Separation
The right to live with parents unless this is deemed incompatible with the child's best interests; the right to maintain contact with both parents; the State to provide information when separation results from State action.

Article 10: Family Reunification
The right to leave or enter any country for family reunification and to maintain contact with both parents.

Article 11: Illicit Transfer and Non-Return
The State to combat the illicit transfer and non-return of children abroad.

Article 12: Free Expression of Opinion
The child's right to express an opinion in matters affecting the child and to have that opinion heard.

Article 13: Freedom of Information
The right to seek, receive and impart information through any media.

Article 14: Freedom of Thought, Conscience and Religion
The right to determine and practise any belief; the State to respect the rights of parents or guardians to provide direction in the exercise of this right.

Article 15: Freedom of Association
The right to freedom of association and freedom of peaceful assembly.

Article 16: Protection of Privacy
The right to protection from arbitrary or unlawful interference with privacy, family, home or correspondence, or attacks on honour or reputation.

Article 17: Media and Information
The State to ensure access to information and material from a diversity of national and international sources.

Article 18: Parental Responsibility
The State to recognize the principle that both parents are responsible for the upbringing of their children and that parents or guardians have primary responsibility; the State to assist parents or guardians in this responsibility and ensure the provision of child care for eligible working parents.

Article 19: Abuse and Neglect
The State to protect children from all forms of abuse, neglect and exploitation by parents or others, and to undertake preventive and treatment programs in this regard.

Article 20: Children without Families
The right to receive special protection and assistance from the State when deprived of family environment and to be provided with alternative care, such as foster placement or Kafala of Islamic Law, adoption or institutional placement.

Article 21: Adoption
The State to regulate the process of adoption (including inter country adoption), where it is permitted.

Article 22: Refugee Children
The State to ensure protection and assistance to children who are refugees or are seeking refugee status, and to cooperate with competent organizations providing such protection and assistance.

Article 23: Disabled Children
The right of disabled children to special care and training designed to help achieve self-reliance and a full and decent life in society.

Article 24: Health Care
The right to the highest attainable standard of health and access to medical services; the State to attempt to diminish infant and child mortality, combat disease and malnutrition, ensure health care for expectant mothers, provide access to health education, develop preventive health care and abolish harmful traditional practices.

Article 25: Periodic Review
The right of children placed by the State for reasons of care, protection or treatment to have all aspects of that placement reviewed regularly.

Appendices

Article 26: Social Security
The right, where appropriate, to benefit from social security or insurance.

Article 27: Standard of Living
The right to an adequate standard of living, the State to assist parents who cannot meet this responsibility and to try to recover maintenance for the child from persons having financial responsibility, both within the State and abroad.

Article 28: Education
The right to education; the State to provide free and compulsory primary education, ensure equal access to secondary and higher education and ensure that school discipline reflects the child's human dignity.

Article 29: Aims of Education
The States Parties' agreement that education be directed at developing the child's personality and talents; preparing the child for responsible life in a free society; developing respect for the child's parents, basic human rights, the natural environment and the child's own cultural and national values and those of others.

Article 30: Children of Minorities
The right of children of minority communities and indigenous populations to enjoy their own culture, practise their own religion and use their own language.

Article 31: Leisure and Recreation
The right to leisure, play and participation in cultural and artistic activities.

Article 32: Child labour
The right to be protected from economic exploitation and from engaging in work that constitutes a threat to health, education and development; the State to set minimum ages for employment, regulate conditions of employment and provide sanctions for effective enforcement.

Article 33: Drug Abuse
The right to protection from the use of narcotic and psychotropic drugs, and from being involved in their production or distribution.

Article 34: Sexual Exploitation
The right to protection from sexual exploitation and abuse, including prostitution and involvement in pornography.

Article 35: Abduction
The State must make every effort to prevent the sale, trafficking and abduction of children.

Article 36: Other Forms of Exploitation
The right to protection from all forms of exploitation not already covered in articles 32, 33, 34 and 35.

Article 37: Tor ture and Deprivation of Liberty
The right to protection from torture, cruel treatment or punishment, unlawful arrest or deprivation of liberty. It is not lawful to use capital punishment or life imprisonment without the possibility of release on a person below 18.

Article 38: Armed Conflicts
State Parties should take all feasible measures to ensure that children under 15 years of age have no direct part in hostilities. No child below 15 should be recruited into the armed forces.

Article 39: Rehabilitative Care
Child victims of armed conflicts, torture, neglect, maltreatment or exploitation have the right to receive appropriate treatment for their recovery and social reintegration.

Article 40: Administration of Juvenile Justice
A child in conflict with the law has the right to treatment which promotes the child's sense of dignity and worth, takes the child's age into account and aims at his or her reintegration into society.